Rex, Abyssinian and Turkish Cats

Rex, Abyssinian and Turkish Cats

ALISON E. ASHFORD

AND

GRACE POND F.Z.S.

ARCO PUBLISHING COMPANY, INC.

New York

Published 1974 by Arco Publishing Company, Inc.
219 Park Avenue South, New York, N.Y. 10003

Library of Congress Catalog Card Number 73-82327

ISBN 0-668-03356-8

Printed in Great Britain

Contents

Acknowledgements

The Authors and Publishers would like to give acknowledgement and thanks to the following for their help:—

Ann Cumbers (photographs)
Derek Davis (photographs)
George Ellis (photographs)
The G.C.C.F. for Standards and Points
Sonia Halliday (Turkish cats)
Boyd A. Langman, B.V.Sc., M.R.C.V.S.
Laura Lushington (Turkish Cats)
Edith Menezes (Abyssinian Cats)
Dr. Scheur-Karpin (German Rex)
Messrs. Sloman and Pettit (photographs)
Roy Robinson, M.I. (Biology)
The late Brian Stirling-Webb (Rex)
Mable Tracy (U.S.A.)
The late John Trevor (Turkish Cats)
C. Westrich (photographs)
and last but not least, our patient Families!

INTRODUCTION

As an ex-zoologist and professional science writer, I must whole-heartedly recommend this book to anyone interested in cats. It is most refreshing to find a professional breeder who is not only able to talk so well from experience about the proper care of this fascinating new breed and who has also been concerned with them from the earliest days, but who also writes so clearly and with such understanding about biology and genetics.

JOHN NEWELL,
B.B.C. European Science Correspondent.

REFLECTIONS ON A CURLY-REX

Slender and lithe
Hallmark of Ra;
Your noble head
praised afar.

Joy of the Nile
Regal and proud
your curly coat
a puzzling shroud.

Hail to your grandee
Cat-goddess of old;
Await the lute-players
Your tale to unfold.

K. A. SWALLOW
Boston, U. S. A.

Annelida Curly Coon—Cornish Rex Cat in stalking mood. Breeder and Owner—Mrs. A. Ashford   *Photographer Anne Cumbers*

1   History of Cornish Rex Cats

In the early hours of a summer morning in 1950, in an old farmhouse on Bodmin Moor in Cornwall, a young tortoiseshell cat gave birth to five kittens. As the owner, Mrs. Ennismore, tidied up the purring mother and her young family she was unaware that this was an historic moment for the Cat Fancy.

On close examination, one of the new-born kittens, a pretty red-and-white male, appeared to have a closely-curled coat! Thinking that it was a result of the fur being still wet Mrs. Ennismore paid little attention to the fact. But as the kitten grew, the curls remained. Even the whiskers were curled, giving the kitten a quaint 'old-man' look. For some years there had been reports of curly cats in Cornwall, but this was the first kitten actually to be recorded.

The other kittens went to new homes, but Kallibunker, as the curly-coated boy was named, became the special pet. Mrs. Ennismore, who had bred Rex rabbits, realised that this was possibly a new feline mutation and asked her veterinary surgeon for guidance. She was put in touch with the late Mr. A. C. Jude, the geneticist, who became deeply interested in this rare cat, which he suggested should be called a Rex cat.

On his advice she mated Kallibunker to his mother and the mating resulted in the birth of two Rex kittens and a plain-coated female. This mating was repeated and again Rex kittens were born.   9

Kallibunker—First Cornish Rex with Poldhu (only Blue-Cream) and
another Cornish Rex   *Photographer George W. F. Ellis*

Unfortunately, soon after this Kallibunker died, but his son, Poldhu, a beautiful blue-cream and white Rex, was kept as a stud and was mated to his mother, his grandmother and all relatives. As a result, a number of Rex kittens were born, but, possibly due to the rapidly-increasing number of cats and also to the continued close inbreeding, they lacked stamina and many died.

However, Poldhu was mated to his daughter, a self-blue Rex from a subsequent litter. This cat, 'Lamorna Cove' was exported to America where she founded the Rex breed, as she gave birth to four Rex kittens. Her half-brother, the red Rex 'Pendennis Castle', was exported to the U.S. at the same time.

Poldhu was not only rare because he was a Rex, but also because he was a blue-cream – and a blue-cream male is as rare as a tortoise-shell male. When they are found they are usually sterile. Geneticists decided to perform a small operation to take a sample of tissue from Poldhu in the hope of discovering more about the reasons why a blue-cream male should be sterile. Alas, contrary to expectations, the small operation made Poldhu sterile and, worst of all, the sample of tissue was mislaid. This was a bitter disappointment to scientists and to Mr. Stirling-Webb, the well-known English experimental cat breeder, who had meanwhile purchased Poldhu in the hopes of furthering this rare breed by careful outcrossing.

Fortunately there was still a fertile Rex son of Kallibunker, a cream-and-white male which Mrs. Ennismore had given to her veterinary surgeon. This cat was christened 'Champagne Chas' and was loaned to Mr. Stirling-Webb, so that the planned breeding could go ahead.

Mr. Stirling-Webb gathered a small group of enthusiastic breeders around him and they all mated queens to the aptly-named Champagne Chas. The females used in these matings were Burmese and short-haired British cats and by 1965 these Gene 1 (or Cornish) Rex cats were beginning to lose their fine-boned foreign look and to resemble more closely the type of the British pedigree cat.

As was to be expected, all the kittens born from the first out-cross matings were plain-coated in varying colours. When they reached maturity, they were either mated back to their sire, or to one another, and the Rex kittens were born in an average ratio of one Rex to three plain-coated kittens.

Poldhu—World's only known Blue-Cream Male. Cornish Rex Son of Kallibunker
Photographer George W. F. Ellis   11

To avoid too close in-breeding, these first Rex kittens were mostly out-crossed again, and so, 21 years after the appearance of the first Cornish Rex, these cats are still comparatively rare.

Because the Cornish Rex were losing their distinctive 'foreign' look, Mr. Stirling-Webb advised me to import a Rex cat from Canada. After much correspondence, I chose Riovista Kismet, a self-blue Cornish Rex bred by Miss Jeanne Jeffrey of Calgary, Alberta. He was a great-great-great grandson of Kallibunker. He had a wonderfully lithe muscular body, superb head and even ripple waves.

Of course Kismet had to spend six months in quarantine. We visited him weekly, and felt that his name was well-chosen. Kismet means 'Fate' and it seemed a happy fate that had brought him to Annelida.

By the time he was released from quarantine he was fully mature and very eager for a mate. His first mate was Annelida Curly Coon, an experienced queen who was willing and tolerant. Their kittens surpassed our wildest hopes and in the next four years Kismet had brought back the desired type to the Cornish Rex. At the end of four years his name appeared in practically all the Cornish Rex pedigrees and because he was no longer getting stud-work we had

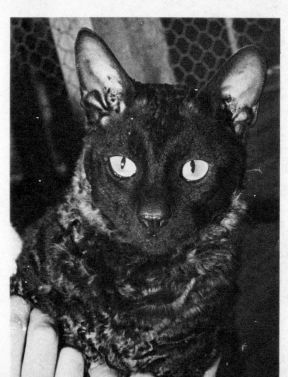

Champion Watermill Othello. Smoke Cornish Rex. Owned by Mrs. Harrison. Bred by M Codrington

12

Britain's first White Cornish Rex. Kittens—Annelida Sparkling Snow and Annelida
Candytuft. Breeder and owner—Mrs. Ashford   *Photographer Anne Cumbers*

Annelida Silver Cascade. 3-month old Cornish Rex Kitten. Breeder—Mrs. A. Ashford.
Owner: Mrs. Lipscombe   *Photographer Anne Cumbers*

him neutered and he became the loved pet of a lonely couple. I have found that it is impossible to keep a neutered stud with breeding queens, as they resent his presence and will attack him without provocation.

We now have one of Kismet's grand-sons at stud, so the desired type is still retained.

Gradually all the colours have been introduced into the Cornish Rex. After four years of out-crossing to Miss Codrington's white short-haired queen Heartsease Seraphina I succeeded in breeding the 'first ever' pair of white Cornish Rex. These cats became immensely popular, but we were heart-broken to lose the male, Annelida Sparkling Snow, from leukaemia. He was only 16 months old and he left a gap that will never be filled.

Now that Rex are officially recognised by the G.C.C.F., there is a constant demand for them, and a recent popularity poll named Cornish Rex as being next in popularity to the Siamese. This poll was carried out in 1970 by Petfoods Ltd., one of Britain's leading manufacturers of canned animal foods.

2 Litters—White Cornish Rex and Black Devon Rex. Owned and bred by Mrs. Ashford　　　　　　　　　　*Photographer Anne Cumbers*

Fionagh Ashford with two typical Devon Rex Kittens—Annelida
Calidor and Annelida Sea-Witch   *Photographer Derek Davis*

2 History of Devon Rex Cats

By 1960 Rex cats were beginning to gain some publicity, and
journalists were using photos of them under the caption 'poodle-Cat'
or even 'the Coodle'. One of these photos was seen by a Miss Cox,
living in Buckfastleigh, Devon. In spite of being disabled, due to
injuries sustained in an Exeter air raid, she was able to breed
dachshunds and to be of active help to the R.S.P.C.A.

For some time Miss Cox had befriended a stray tortie-and-white
female cat, who spent her time wandering in the fields. At this time
Miss Cox lived quite close to a disused tin mine, in which wandered
a wild curly-coated male cat. Miss Cox says that this cat was very
beautiful with masses of tight curls and ringlets up his tail.

In due course the tortie-and-white queen became friendly with the
curly tom and the result was a litter of kittens born in the field at the
foot of Miss Cox's garden. One of these kittens, a male, was curly-
coated like his father.

Miss Cox kept this kitten, naming him Kirlee. He grew to be
extremely affectionate and intelligent, following her like a dog. One
of his favourite tricks was to walk a tight rope, wagging his tail for
approval as he did so.

When Miss Cox saw the photo of the Rex kitten she realised that
she probably had a cat which could be valuable to the breeders who
were concentrating on establishing a new breed, and she contacted
Mr. Stirling-Webb, of the Rex 'group'.

Kirlee—First Devon Rex (Taken 1963)

Photograph Daily Express

The discovery of Kirlee caused great excitement among the Rex breeders, who persuaded Miss Cox to part with her pet. It must have been a great sacrifice to give up the kitten which had proved such a loving and amusing companion for nearly a year. Every attempt was made to capture the wild Rex, but he evaded each attempt. As far as is known he still roams the mine, but remains a legend to the people of Buckfastleigh.

Naturally, Mr. Stirling-Webb assumed that, since Kirlee came from a county so close to Cornwall, he would be of a similar blood-line, a genotype, to the original Kallibunker. So Kirlee was mated to one of the Rex descendants of Kallibunker and the first litter eagerly awaited, as this would be the first pure Rex generation to be born.

But nature has a habit of having the last word and all the kittens born were straight-haired or 'plain'. Since no definite conclusion could be reached at the result of only one mating, this same mating was repeated and also several of the Rex queens were mated to Kirlee.

However, each time the resulting kittens were 'plain', and it became obvious that Kirlee was of a different genotype, a new type of Rex. It was necessary to differentiate between the two types, and so Kallibunker's descendants were named Gene 1 (Cornish) Rex and Kirlee was known as Gene 2 (Devon) Rex.

With Kirlee it was now necessary to follow the same breeding pattern as had been taken with Kallibunker, but since his mother was no longer alive his daughter had to be mated back to him. Several of his daughters were put with him and in the resulting litters Devon Rex kittens were born in approximately the ratio of 1:1, although with this type the ratio of Rex seemed slightly higher than the expected average.

One of Kirlee's first daughters, Broughton Golden Rain, was bred by Mrs. P. Hughes out of a Cornish Rex queen. This kitten was sent to Mrs. Lauder and when mature was mated back to her father. She produced a black short-haired female, a red short-haired male and a blue-cream Rex, a fascinating little creature, resembling a bush-baby in its expression. The little black female, Belhaven Zarakhat, came to live with us, and was soon to become the mother of our first Devon Rex kittens.

At a later date Golden Rain was mated to a Cornish male, and two Rex and two 'plain' resulted from this mating. Golden Rain was of great interest to geneticists, as she was the only hybrid then known to carry both Rex genes. Unfortunately, she died when her second litter was still young, but it has now been proved that our Zarakhat is also a carrier of both genes.

Ch. Sunbronze Danny Boy, Devon Rex. Breeder—Mrs. P. Harrison. Owner—Mrs. G. Fisher

17

Kirlee is now neutered and is the adored pet of friends of Mr. Stirling-Webb. The fact that I bought Broughm, one of Kirlee's sons, is a tribute to the tremendous personality of these cats. I visited Mrs. Sedgefield of Esher one day in 1962, and saw Du-Bu-Debbie, a young tortoiseshell, with her litter of Rex and 'plain' kittens. One kitten jumped into my arms from the floor, and literally refused to be put down. I tried to turn away, but loud purring and a wagging tail were the prelude to another amorous leap. This was Broughm, then six months old. I could not then really afford the price of a Rex kitten, but I could not leave him. So I rashly wrote a cheque on my housekeeping account and phoned home to warn my husband to have a bed ready for the new acquisition. I was given a somewhat cold reception when I arrived home, but Broughm's charm soon convinced the family that it would be worth eating bread and cheese for the next month.

Broughm was used in a number of experimental breeding trials, and Mrs. Evely of Old Coulsdon was successful in breeding a Burmese Rex, the result of mating a Burmese queen to Broughm, and then mating a brother to a sister from the resulting litter.

Devon Rex. Berrileon Augustus. Owned and bred by Mrs. Lyon
Photographer Derek Davis

Ch. Annelida Icicle (Devon Rex) Britain's first Champion White Rex
Owned and bred by Mrs. Ashford   *Photographer Ann Cumbers*

Together with Mrs. Lidyard of Charing, Kent, I attempted to breed a 'Siamese-Rex'; that is, a Rex with Siamese coat pattern. Two Siamese queens, a Blue Point and a Lilac Point, were mated to Broughm. I kept a black hybrid daughter of the Blue Point mating, Mrs. Casswell kept the male, and Mrs. Lidyard kept a male and female hybrid from the Lilac Point mating. From matings of my hybrid to her litter brother I succeeded only in obtaining solid-coloured Rex, Siamese type kittens, and hybrids. However, when Mrs. Lidyard mated her Siamese-Rex hybrid female and also a Burmese-Rex hybrid female to her hybrid male she succeeded in getting a Seal-Pointed Rex in both litters. This caused great excitement in the Cat Fancy and the kittens were photographed by several newspapers. Mallorca Sicat, the little Seal-Pointed Rex male, came to live with me and became well-known through a brief appearance on the B.B.C. Television programme 'Blue Peter'.

When mature he was mated to his Si-Rex half-sister, who presented Mrs. Lidyard with three beautiful Seal-Pointed Si-Rex. Mrs. Knight of Cornwall bought Annelida Pixie Poppet, a Devon queen carrying Siamese genes. She was mated to Mrs. Lidyard's hybrid male and produced two Si-Rex and two hybrids.

Naturally, the first Si-Rex tended to have too straight a profile, but thanks largely to the efforts made by Mr. Wakeford and Mrs. Worthy, Si-Rex with true Devon type are now appearing on the show benches.

The various possibilities of Rex combinations seem limitless, but housing-space and finances prove to be the chief obstacle to most keen breeders.

3   Elementary Genetics

The study of genetics is very specialised, and one on which I am certainly not qualified to write. However, to breed intelligently, and so achieve the desired results, it is necessary to know a little about genetics and how they apply to every-day breeding.

Reproduction is the forming of a new individual from the fusion of a female egg-cell and a male sperm. All cells of the animal body contain chromosomes which carry the genes or characters of that individual. Thus the egg-cell and the sperm must carry only half the normal number of chromosomes so that on fusing they produce a cell called the zygote, which again contains the full number of chromosomes. It is apparent therefore that the new individual inherits half its chromosomes (and therefore characteristics) from the father and half from the mother.

These characteristics or genes exist in pairs called 'alleles'. The two genes in a pair may be similar, in which case they are called 'homozygous', or they may be dissimilar and are called 'heterozygous'.

Gregor Mendel, an Augustine Father, from Brno, was the first man to prove the theory of heredity, and since then (1900) the law of heredity has been known as 'Mendel's Law'.

Mendel proved that if two genetically differing individuals are mated the offspring will be heterozygous. But if the resulting offspring are crossed with each other the original types will again appear, as pure as the original, but only in certain proportions of the total progeny.

In a certain pair of genes one is dominant to the other, known as the recessive gene. Therefore an individual that shows a recessive character must have a homozygous allele for that character, and these must always breed true when mated together.

A homozygous dominant mated with another homozygous dominant will, of course, produce only dominants. A homozygous dominant mated with a homozygous recessive will produce progeny that are phenotypically (i.e. in outward appearance) 'dominants', but which will all be heterozygous for the recessive gene. When this generation is mated *inter se* the resulting proportion will be in the

Mendelian average of one recessive to three dominants, and the dominants will be heterozygous. The mating of a heterozygous dominant with a homozygous recessive gives a ratio of 1:1.

The terms usually used to describe genetical events are as follows:
1. The generation from which a particular experiment is begun is called the P_1 or Parental Generation.
2. The offspring of this generation are called the first filial generation or F_1.
3. Those resulting from the crossing of two F_1 individuals are called the second filial generation or F_2.

The following chart may be of some help to novice Rex breeders as it shows at a glance approximately the proportion of Rex one may expect from certain matings.

RR = Plain-coated cat
rr = Rex-coated cat
Rr = Plain-coated hybrid Rex cat

Capital letters represent dominant genes; small letters recessive genes.

P_1 generation: RR × rr
F_1 generation: Rr Rr   Rr Rr (all plain-coated hybrid Rex)
Back-Cross   Rr × rr
    to Recessive   Rr rr   Rr rr (2 Rex, 2 plain-coated hybrid Rex)
F_1 generation: Rr × Rr
F_2 generation: RR Rr   Rr rr (1 plain-coated cat, 2 hybrid Rex,
                            1 Rex)
Recessive to   rr × rr
    Recessive   rr rr   rr rr (all Rex)

While there are genes for every character, in Rex breeding we are chiefly interested in those concerned with coat and colour.

The Rex Coat
According to a paper published by A. C. Jude and A. G. Searle (1956) a normal cat has four layers to its coat:
(1) The outer, straight guard-hairs
(2) The awn-hairs of the over-fur
(3) The intermediate awned down-hairs
(4) The down-hairs of the under-fur, which are evenly thin and crimped

At that time samples of hair from Rex cats showed that the Rex had no guard-hairs, no awn-hairs, no awned intermediate down, but only down-hairs. However, microscopic examination in later generations of Rex of both genes show occasional guard-hairs.

Annelida Curly Coon.
Cornish Rex Cat.
Owner and breeder—
Mrs. A. Ashford
*Photographer Anne
Cumbers*

Annelida Spotted Devon Rex Kittens—the first in Britain. *Photographer Sloman & Pettitt*

Sayonara Lilac Frosting (Female) and Sayonara Lilac Time (male).
First Lilac Pointed Devon Rex Kittens. Bred by Mrs. Glenda Worthy
Photographer Arthur Sidey, Daily Mirror

Rex cats are now bred in all colours, and the novice breeder can learn only from others or from test-matings which colours will be dominant.

The most important point to remember in Rex breeding is that the Rex gene is a recessive and will always breed true. Therefore a Rex mated to a Rex will only produce Rex. But there is a pitfall here. The Rex × Rex mating *must* be between two cats of the same genotype. If a Cornish Rex cat is mated to a Devon Rex cat the resulting generation will all be straight-coated. These cats should not be used for breeding, as the G.C.C.F. has ruled that Cornish Rex should NOT be mated to Devon Rex.

Most 'new' breeds of cats are the result of planned cross-matings between two established breeds. The Rex cat, however, is a natural mutation, and we can only assume at the present time that its breeding will follow Mendel's Law. The immediate future will be of immense interest to all Rex fanciers. The names of the original pioneer Rex breeders will always be remembered:- Mesdames Aitken, Hardy, Hughes, Lauder, Watts and Mr. Stirling-Webb.

4   Characteristics— Types— of Rex Cats G.C.C.F. Standard of Points

The popular press has named the Rex cats 'Poodle Cats'. This is particularly apt, even if undignified, as these cats have all the intelligence of a poodle, as well as the curly coat. There is, however, a considerable difference in the two genotypes, in character as well as in appearance.

Cornish Rex are very quiet, even when in season, and though they love to be included in all the events of the day, they are content to be the onlookers. Not so with the Devon Rex, though. These are extremely lively and somewhat demanding cats, hating to be ignored. If I am busy in the kitchen I try to ignore the persistent voices of my Devon kittens. But if I fail to answer their cries I soon feel an affectionate patting on my leg, or if this does not interrupt me one of the kittens will take a sure-footed leap on to my shoulder.

The early generations of both types of Rex were soft-voiced, even when calling, which I found pleasant after my vociferous Siamese. However, with the introduction of Siamese into the Rex pedigree some of the voices are becoming louder, more like their pure Siamese relatives.

The original Cornish Rex, Kallibunker, was of a definitely modified foreign type. In 1965 the Colourpoint Rex-Coated and Any Other Variety Club, the original Club to cater for Rex cats, drew up a provisional standard of points for both types of Rex, and it was then decided that Cornish should ideally have modified foreign type.

The Devon Rex have a very marked 'foreign' appearance and their type has remained unchanged since the advent of Kirlee in 1960. This Rex is so very like the cats of ancient Egypt which were worshipped as goddesses. The picture of the small statue of Bastet, now in the British Museum, shows this likeness when compared with photographs of Broughm and Champion Annelida Icicle.

Breeders have unanimously decided to keep this fascinating type, and the official G.C.C.F Standard allots 60 points for general 'type'.

Because of their intelligence, Rex cats train easily to a lead, and are happiest when accompanying their owner for walks or on a car journey. My stud, Icicle, delighted to go with us for a drink at the

25

'local', where he would wait patiently for a few coveted crisps. When he grew older we seldom took him out, as like all good studs the scent of another male aroused his fury, and most pubs have a pet tom prowling round the corners.

Diet for Rex cats will be dealt with in a separate chapter. But I must mention that these lovable cats have the most fanciful tastes in food. They will go wild with joy if offered small tit-bits of Stilton cheese, smoked salmon or milk chocolate. When my friends drop in for coffee, it is a usual sight to see Champion Annelida Lucia (Cornish) carefully removing a chocolate biscuit from the plate on the table. She carries it gently to the corner of the room and is then happy for the rest of the morning.

Since Rex cats have only down hairs in their coats, they fare badly in a heavy shower of rain. They are extremely hardy, going out in all weathers, but a heavy shower will quickly soak them and they will return home a sorry sight. In spite of this they adore water and will spend many half-hours playing under a dripping tap, or dipping a paw into a bowl of water, then shaking it, watching intently where the drops fall, and then pouncing on them.

The coats of Rex cats are very soft to the touch and, like poodles, they do not moult as other cats do. Small balls of fluff do collect on them, but are quickly brushed away with a soft brush. A few Devon Rex cats have so little fur that some people have named them 'hairless cats'. This hairlessness is a fault, and one that is being bred out by careful selective breeding.

After several years of experimental breeding it is now obvious that any breed of cat can be Rexed. At the present time this needs careful in-breeding, using a brother × sister mating of the F_1 generation, but as there are more breeders out-crossing to known breeds there will be a greater choice of studs carrying the required genes.

Rex cats make devoted mothers. Indeed, they seem happiest when surrounded by a brood of bouncing kittens, though it is sad to see their bewilderment when it is time for the kittens to go to their new homes. I always 'stagger' the departure of the kittens, and in this way the mother becomes resigned to their loss. Usually, too, nature takes a hand: the queen starts to call for a mate and so the whole cycle starts again.

It is an established rule of the English G.C.C.F. that, until there are four clear generations of a new breed it cannot be granted a separate breed number. For this reason, though all fanciers knew the Rex cat, it was not officially granted recognition until 1967. The Rex cats then had Championship status – the 'first-ever' Cornish Cham-

Senty-Twix Cornish Rex. Owned and bred by Mrs. Hardy.

Photographer Derek Davis

pion being Mrs. Bygrave's Noend Krinkle, and the first Devon Champion was Mrs. Genty's Amharic Curly Katie, bred by Mrs. Knight.

In 1964, largely due to the enthusiasm of Mrs. Madge Shrouder (breeder of Hassan cats) the Rex Cat Club was formed, and the Colourpoint Rex-Coated and A.O.V. Club now work together, to the mutual benefit of the Rex breed. We are proud that Annelida cats were the second to have bred four generations of pure Rex.

STANDARD OF POINTS FOR

CORNISH REX, BREED 33

Coat: Short, thick and plushy, without guard hairs and should curl, wave or ripple, particularly on back and tail. Whiskers and eyebrows crinkled and of good length. All coat colours acceptable, but any white markings must be symmetrical, except in Tortoiseshell and White.

27

Head: Medium wedge. Head length about one-third greater than the maximum width, narrowing to a strong chin. The skull to be flat. In profile a straight line to be seen from the centre of forehead to end of nose.

Eyes: Oval shaped, medium in size, colouring in keeping with coat colour.

Ears: Large. Set rather high on head, wide at base, tapering to rounded tops and well covered with fine fur.

Body and legs: Body hard and muscular, slender and of medium length. Legs long and straight, giving an overall appearance of being high on the legs. Paws small and oval.

Tail: Long, fine and tapering, well covered with curly fur.

Scale of points:

Coat	50
Head	5
Eyes	5
Ears	10
Body and legs	25
Tail	5
	100 Total

Faults:
1. Asymmetrical white markings, except in Tortoiseshell and White.
2. Shaggy or too short a coat.
3. Bare patches to be considered a fault in kittens and a serious fault in cats.
4. British type head, or too long a wedge.
5. Small ears.
6. Cobby body.
7. Lack of firm muscles.
8. Short or bare tail.

STANDARD OF POINTS FOR

DEVON REX, BREED 33A

Coat: Very short and fine, wavy and soft, without guard hairs. Whiskers and eyebrows crinkled, rather coarse and of medium length. All coat colours, except bi-colours, acceptable. Any white markings other than in Tortoiseshell and White will be considered a fault.

Head: Wedge-shaped with face full cheeked. Short muzzle with a

Actress Carmen Dene with her favourite cat, Britain's first white Cornish Rex: Annelida Candytuft
Photographer Derek Shuff

strong chin and whisker break. Nose with a strongly marked stop. Forehead curving back to a flat skull.

Eyes: Wide set, large, oval shaped and sloping towards outer edges of ears. Colour in keeping with coat colour, or except in Si-Rex, chartreuse, green or yellow.

Ears: Large, set rather low, very wide at base, tapering to rounded tops and well covered with fine fur. With or without ear muffs.

Body, legs and neck: Body hard and muscular, slender and of medium length, broad in chest carried high on long slim legs, with length of hind legs emphasised. Paws small and oval. Neck slender.

Tail: Long, fine and tapering, well covered with short fur.

Scale of points:		
Coat	40	
Head	15	
Eyes	5	
Ears	10	
Body, legs and neck	25	
Tail	5	
	100	Total

Faults: 1. Straight or shaggy coat.
2. Any white markings, other than Tortoiseshell and White.
3. Bare patches to be considered a fault in kittens and a serious fault in cats.
4. Narrow, long or British type head.
5. Cobby body.
6. Lack of firm muscles.
7. Small or high set ears.
8. Short, bare or bushy tail.

Footnote: Many Devon Rex cats have down on the underparts. This should not be misinterpreted as bareness.

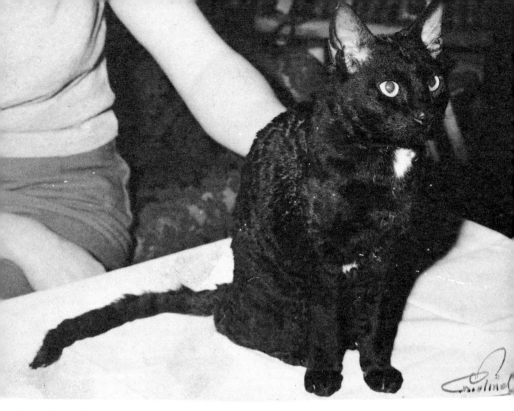

Laamchen, First German Rex. Owned by Dr. Scheur Karpin of East Berlin

Photographer Ch. Polinet

5   Mutations

(1) *German*

It was not until Kallibunker's pictures began to appear in the newspapers that German breeders informed their English counterparts of a German Rex mutation. This first Rex was found as long ago as 1946. Laamchen, as this black Rex was named, was found by Dr. Scheur-Karpin of East Berlin. She became a great pet and had numerous mongrel litters. When she was about 10 years old she was mated to her plain 'black son' and in 1957 the first Rex litter in Germany was born. That same year she was mated to a domestic short-haired red male and their son 'Blackie 2' was then kept as a stud.

In 1958 two Rex females were born and in 1960 both male and female Rex were born. One black Rex male, Christopher Columbus, was exported to the U.S. to Mrs. J. O'Shea. This lovely cat, closely resembling our own Devon cats, founded the German strain in America and has gained his championship.

A daughter and grand-daughter of Lammchen were flown to Mrs. Muckenhaupt of Massachusetts, U.S., early in 1961 and about   31 the same time another daughter went to Paris.

Several German breeders are now interested in the Rex cat, and are considering importing one of the English mutations. Meanwhile, in Maryland, U.S.A., Mrs. Mable Tracy has mated Cornish Rex to German Rex several times, and each time all the kittens have been Rex-coated (*Cats Magazine*, September, 1970). It must have been very exciting to find that the two mutations are compatible, although this was predicted by the well-known geneticist, Roy Robinson, after microscopic examination of both types of fur.

It is strange that the first Rex cats to appear in several countries seem to have been born around the 1950s. We have asked several scientific friends for a possible explanation, but there does not appear to be one. Of course, pessimists say solemnly 'Oh, it must be the result of an atomic bomb,' but nobody seriously believes this. It seems more feasible that Rex cats were born in earlier years, but since the Rex mutation seems to occur in domestic cats rather than pedigree the owners destroyed them as being 'diseased'.

(2) *American*

It is interesting to hear that an ordinary domestic cat gave birth to a Rex kitten in Plainsville, Ohio, in 1953. The owner, Miss Hedderman, kept this kitten, 'Toni', but unfortunately he died of an

Rio Vista Kismet—The first Rex cat to be imported to England (Cornish Rex) Breeder—Miss J. Jeffrey, Calgary, Canada. Owner— Mrs. A. E. Ashford   *Photographer Derek Davis*

Canadian Champion Annelida Calidor, Devon Rex, son of Broughm

infection at an early age. However, the dam had three more Rex kittens from similar matings and these were all reared. But, as all breeders know, the breeding of a new strain is a costly business and Miss Hedderman was unable to carry on and this valuable mutation is thought to be lost.

Mrs. M. Stringham of Warrenton, Oregon, tells in *All-Pets Magazine* of February 1964 of how her calico domestic queen gave birth to one curly-coated black-and-white kitten in a litter of normally-coated kittens. Naturally there was great excitement about this, as Mrs. Stringham was already a well-known catbreeder. She contacted Mr. Jude in England and after seeing photographs of the kitten he confirmed that she was a Rex, named Kinky Marcella. She is the founder of the American Rex. Mrs. Blancheri and Mrs. Weiss of the famous Daz-Zling prefix were already breeding Rex from the first English import, but Mrs. Stringham, knowing that English and American Rex would probably be incompatible, decided to outcross Marcella to a blue-hybrid Rex. This mating produced five blue-and-black hybrids. A blue son was mated back to his mother and Mrs. Stringham was thrilled to find that 50 per cent of the resulting litter were Rex.

Since then she has carried out other outcrosses and back-crosses and always the proportion of Rex has been higher than the expected ratio.

Rex cats were soon allowed to compete for championships at American shows, although only two cat federations (similar to our G.C.C.F.) recognise them as a breed. These two federations are U.C.F. and A.C.F.A.

The most significant point about all these foreign mutations is that regardless of the type of the original parent the mutation always has the large ears and long, elegant body and tail, that we know in England as 'foreign type'.

Long-haired Rex Cats

The gene for long hair in cats is a recessive one and may remain hidden for many generations, until it meets its allele.

The first recorded long-haired Rex was a surprise, being born in a litter bred by Mr. Stirling-Webb. The sire was the original Devon Rex cat 'Kirlee', and the dam a hybrid Rex bred by Mrs. Watts. This mating produced normal Rex-hybrids, and a long-haired Rex. There was no history of a long-haired cat in the pedigrees, but it is possible that Kirlee carried the gene for long hair and that therefore the hybrid did also.

This kitten was very attractive when young, with long tight ringlets, but as it matured the coat became untidy with an unkempt look, even though the cat was brushed frequently.

In 1965 a Mrs. Gilliam of Surrey mated her long-haired Blue to a well-known long-haired Blue stud. There were three kittens in the resulting litter, one of which had an 'odd' coat. Mrs. Gilliam had not then heard of Rex, but when she visited the National Show she saw some of our Rex cats, and told me of this strange kitten, then a bonny young male at four months.

Shortly after this she brought the kitten to me and there seemed no doubt that this kitten was a Rex mutation. The fur around the legs and on the tummy was in close ringlets, but on the back it had a merely 'frizzy' look. I took sample cuttings of the fur and sent them to Mr. Roy Robinson. He examined the hairs microscopically and then wrote that this kitten was undoubtedly a Rex mutation, as the hairs were definitely curled and showed the expected lack of guard-hairs.

Mr. Stirling-Webb was then consulted and he advised that this kitten should be mated back to his mother, when the usual ratio of 1:1 Rex should result. Unfortunately, due to the owner's illness the experiment was never carried out.

From America came the news that in 1965 in California a long-haired curly-coated tortoiseshell female and her long-haired curly-coated son had been discovered. The Tortie female was mated to a

German x Cornish Rex Kitten No. 1. Owned and bred by Mrs. Tracy
Pan Prints Cattery

German x Cornish Rex Kitten No. 2. Owned and bred by Mrs. Tracy
Pan Prints Cattery   35

hybrid Rex carrying Cornish Rex, and the resultant litter were all smooth-coated, proving that this again was a new Rex mutation. The F1 progeny were then mated together and ordinary short-haired Rex kittens were produced. Once again the owners were not able to carry on with their experimental breeding and it is assumed that the long-haired Rex died out.

Because this type of Rex tend to have limp coats, which look untidy, it does not seem likely that they will ever become popular as pets, but it is interesting to know that they can be bred.

Ch. Annelida Smokey Pearl. Devon Rex. Gained award of best Smoke Rex Male in all America 1965. Owner—Miss M. Carroll, Canada. Breeder—Mrs. A. Ashford   *Photographer Derek Davis*

6 History of the Abyssinians and General Characteristics

One of the most striking-looking cats, and differing from all other shorthairs in having a ticked coat, the Abyssinian is included in the 'Foreign' varieties. The term 'Foreign' means a certain type and does not necessarily refer to the country of origin.

There are two recognised varieties, one having fur ruddy brown in colour and the other rich copper red. The type is the same for both; that is, a slender body, a long and pointed head, but not so wedge-shaped as that of the Siamese, nor should the sharp tufted ears be quite as big. An Abyssinian should never be large or coarse in size and should have a short fine close coat. The tail should be fairly long and tapering, but not so whip-like as seen in the Siamese. The large expressive eyes may be green, yellow or hazel. Bad faults are white chins and white on the stomach.

In the original variety the ruddy-brown hairs should have tickings of black or dark brown, and the pads should be black, while in the Red the tickings should be of a darker red, and the pads pink. The full standards are given at the end of this chapter.

Abyssinians were recognised in England as long ago as 1882, making them one of the oldest pedigree varieties, but comparatively little has been written about them and their origin is still obscure. Because of the similarity in outline and shape to the statuettes seen in museums, many cat lovers like to accept the theory, alas not authenticated, that these delightful and lovable creatures are the direct descendants of the cats beloved and worshipped by the Egyptians thousands of years ago. Indeed, some owners go so far as to say that they are sure their cats are reincarnations of those early felines. It is a truly charming belief but it must be accepted that the modern specimens of today have resulted solely through years of carefully-planned breeding.

The early writers on pedigree cats differed among themselves as to how the Abyssinians originated. One theory is that a Mrs. Barrett-Lennard brought one from Abyssinia to England in 1868, but there is no written proof of this. It is interesting to note that there were 37

British troops in that country at that time under the command of Sir Robert Napier, sent there to clarify the situation after the Emperor of Abyssinia had been involved in the arrest of a number of Europeans. Apparently on hearing of the presence of the troops he committed suicide, and shortly afterwards the soldiers were recalled home. It is more than likely, knowing the British love of animals, that any unusual-looking cat or kitten would have been brought back with them. It has been said that there are no such cats in Abyssinia, but I find this difficult to believe, having seen in North Africa, and in countries bordering the Mediterranean, also in Greece and the Greek islands, cats with the most distinctive ticked coats and the colouring of the Abyssinians, proving that this coat pattern still appears in Africa and Europe. Admittedly the majority of these cats had tabby markings in some form or another, but so did the early specimens of the breed seen here, and many of the pedigree still have some slight barring. Frances Simpson in *The Book of the Cat* (London, 1903) comments on the fact that the so-called Abyssinian cats of her time bore a 'very striking resemblance to the Egyptian or Caffre cat, and a picture of a painting in her book features an Abyssinian cat with ringed tail and many stripes on the legs. Harrison Weir in his *Our Cats and All About Them* (1889) said that a cross between the English wild cat and a domestic cat had produced kittens similar to those imported from Abyssinia, so there obviously had been some from that country. John Jennings, writing in his *Domestic or Fancy Cats* (London, 1893) thought that 'The Abyssinian promises to increase in popularity, and whether imported or a manufactured cross hardly matters, as it now breeds fairly true to point.' He went on to say that 'no variety has yet rejoiced in such varied names, several countries claiming it as their own'. Harrison Weir commented on the fact that it had been shown under a variety of names, such as Russian, Spanish, Abyssinian, Hare cat, Rabbit cat, and that 'some had gone so far to maintain that it is a cross between the latter and a cat, proving very unmistakably there is nothing, however absurd or impossible, in animal or everyday life, that some people are not ready to credit and believe'. The fact that apparently the early Abyssinians were known by different names may account for the fact that so little is known about them; early researchers failing to realise that this was so, passing over what might have been vital links because of the change of name of the variety.

Several writers give 'Zulu' as the name of Mrs. Barrett-Lennard's cat, but apart from that there is no mention by name of any of the

Brown Abyssinian
with Blue Kitten,
Axum Cleopatra.
Owner and Breeder—
Mrs. Evely
Photographer
Anne Cumbers

Abyssinian Kittens. Bred by Mrs. Menezes

early Abyssinians, which is a great pity. There are, however, a few descriptions, and referring again to the book by John Jennings he wrote in 1893 that 'those who are familiar with the Belgian hare rabbit will have no difficulty in recognising the cat yclept Abyssinian. The fur throughout has for ground colour a rufous red, ticked with chocolate-black; ears, medium-sized and laced with black; and a narrow, well defined stripe of black running longitudinally along the spine, and continuing to the extremity of the tail, is a feature of great importance in a good exhibition specimen. The eye varies in colour, but a bright hazel is generally met with. In size, the Abyssinian resembles the self-coloured English cat. The coat should be very close and soft, the brighter the better, though some are weak in this respect'.

A year or two earlier Harrison Weir, who was responsible for the first standards, said of this 'pretty and interesting variety' that 'it is mostly of a deep brown, ticked with black, somewhat resembling the back of a wild (only not so grey) rabbit. Along the centre of the back, there is a band of black, very slightly interspersed with dark brown hairs. The inner sides of the legs and belly are more of a rufous-orange tint than the body, and are marked in some cases with a few dark patches; but they are best without these marks, and in the exhibition pens it is a point lost. The eyes are deep yellow tinted with green; nose dark red, black-edged; ears rather small, dark brown, with black edges and tips; the pads of the feet are black'. Comparison with the recognised standard given at the end of the chapter will show that apart from the ear size there is very little difference between the early and the present characteristics required.

In spite of this, there was some argument at the beginning of the century as to the name and the colouring required, and for a while they were referred to as 'Bunny cats' or 'Ticked'. Some appeared at the shows with coats of darkish grey, rather than red, and these seemed to have been particularly favoured by Louis Wain, well-known for his humorous cat drawings, but who was also one of the leading cat judges of his day and eventually President of the National Cat Club. Strangely enough, Abyssinians with silver or bluish coats are once again making their appearance at the shows, with several fanciers being interested in breeding them.

Mr. H. C. Brooke, an early enthusiast, considered that the most outstanding Abyssinians at the end of the nineteenth century were 'Sedgemore Peaty' and 'Sedgemore Bottle', bred by Mr. Sam Woodiweiss. He wrote in his small book *The Abyssinian Cat* that 'it is truly remarkable how two such (unrelated) specimens were obtained.

Brown Abyssinian, "Abyseal Jade"
Photographer Anne Cumbers

Abyssinians (Brown). Philos Kittens. Bred by Miss
Scatchard   *Photographer Anne Cumbers*

41

They were very much the colour of a hare'. He eventually was the owner of 'Peaty' until her death.

A cat 'Little Bunny Teedle Tit' took first prize at the 1902 Crystal Palace show, and it was said, although no mention is made of her colour, that she won purely on type although in colour 'she was not the best penned'. Then, as now, white spots were considered faults, but sometimes there were complaints from exhibitors that a dark, almost sooty cat was placed over a better-coloured one 'merely because the latter had about a dozen white hairs on its throat'.

A keen breeder in the early 1900s was Sir Claud Alexander, whose Champion Southampton Red Rust was a constant winner. A Mrs. E. A. Clark showed a number of Abyssinians. One bred by Mrs. Carew-Cox, another well-known fancier, was obviously silver in colour, as her name was Silver Fairy, the sire being Aluminium.

Although always much admired, but perhaps because of the small numbers in the litters, three or four being considered average, with males predominating, the numbers have increased very slowly over the years, and the Abyssinian is still a comparatively rare variety.

At the beginning of the century at one National Cat Club show held at the Crystal Palace, there were 'no fewer than eleven Abyssinians penned – a record number' according to an early writer. At the National Cat Club Show at Olympia in 1970 the number penned was 30, so the rise in 70 years has been far from spectacular. It should be remembered, however, that many more are registered and the majority never appear on the show bench, living happy and carefree lives purely as decorative pets.

To return to the early breeders, Mr. H. C. Brooke worked very hard to improve the variety, and when he gave up Mrs. Carew-Cox took over, and continued to try to popularise them for more than 25 years. Both Mr. Sam Woodiweiss and his son Major Sydney Woodiweiss were keen fanciers, with kittens bearing their prefixes 'Sedgmore' and 'Woodroffe' respectively forming the nucleus of several catteries overseas, including the United States. A Mrs. E. A. Clark's cats became well-known for their constant wins, and a note in *Our Cats* for the issue of July 1912 comments: 'It may interest *O.C.* readers to know that Mrs. Clark's "Ras Dashan" was sire of Mrs. Carew Cox's winning Abyssinian, "Adis Ababa", who took 1st championship cup and specials; thus "Ras Dashan" had to be contented with 2nd prize for the first time in his life. However, Mrs. Clark was delighted at being the breeder of the winning Abyssinian at Richmond, and felt as gratified as if her own pet was the winner.'

Ras Dashan was responsible for a number of prize-winning kittens

Abyssinian Male. Ch. Taishun Leo. Mrs. Menezes
Photographer Anne Cumbers
Brown Abyssinian Kitten. Owned by Mrs. Menezes
Photographer Anne Cumbers

of his time; his achievements at the shows stretched over several years, his progeny laying the foundations of several present-day catteries.

The First World War nearly saw the end of this variety, but Mrs. Carew Cox struggled on to keep the Abyssinians going, helped by Major Sydney Woodiweiss, who in 1929 founded the Abyssinian Cat Club. Mr. and Mrs. H. Basnett became interested in this variety, and several kittens bearing their 'Croham' prefix were sent to the United States.

In 1909, at the Boston Show in the United States, a Miss Jane Cathcart exhibited two, 'Champion Aluminium', presumably an import and the one previously mentioned as the sire of 'Silver Fancy', and Salt, probably Silvers. According to the Cat Fanciers' Association records, a male cat 'Boz Ah Sin', belonging to a Mrs. O. Kildare, was registered in 1917, although born in 1914. Apart from this, without having access to all the records, there appear to have been no other Abyssinians in the United States until Mrs. Gardiner Fiske had two, 'Woodroofe Anthony' and 'Ena', bred by Major Sydney Woodiweiss, sent over from England. They seemed to have been poor breeders, perhaps because they may have been too closely bred, and from several litters only two survived. The male, 'Anthony', was later neutered and kept as a pet, and Mrs. A. Cobb, a famous American breeder with a large cattery, took over 'Ena'. This cat was acquired on breeding terms from her by Mrs. M. Metcalf and Miss M. Hantzmon of Washington, and as there was no male with which to mate her, Champion Ras Seyum was eventually sent out from England by Major Woodiweiss in 1937. He was said to have been an outstanding specimen with a beautiful coat colouring and very good type and apparently the English fanciers were most upset when they learned that such a wonderful cat had left their shores. Further imports followed and these cats were the beginning of the ever-increasing Abyssinian Cat Fancy in the States today. There is still a constant stream of outstanding kittens from Britain to the United States, and in all probability there are far more of this variety in that country now than have ever been seen in Britain. Australia, New Zealand and many other countries, even Abyssinia (now Ethiopia), have imported British stock from time to time.

Just as the variety was beginning to really increase in numbers the Second World War saw the almost cessation of breeding in Britain, with many cats being neutered, others having to be destroyed, and a number being sent to the States for safety. One or two breeders, however, managed to struggle on, and when cat shows started again

Abyssinian (Brown)' 'Philos Cameo''. Owned and bred by Miss Scatchard
Photographer Anne Cumbers

after the War, Miss V. Basnett was able to exhibit several 'Cromham'
cats bred by her mother. Other winning cats of that period included
'Champion Raby Ramphis' bred by Lady Barnard, the 'Bruns-
wyckes' bred by Mrs. Anderson and the 'Merklands' of Lord and
Lady Liverpool. Very soon, too, other fanciers began to make their
mark, notable among them being Mrs. E. Menezes, whose cats and
kittens bearing the 'Taishun' prefix are now world-famous; Mrs.
G. de Udy of the 'Gracefield' prefix, Mrs. L. France of 'Chinki'
fame and Mrs. H. Denham of the 'Frensham' prefix. (The late Mr.
and Mrs. S. Denham were the leading authorities of the day on
Abyssinians and the co-authors of the most informative and now
unobtainable booklet on this variety – *Child of the Gods.*) Miss
F. Bone's 'Nigella' cats began to make their appearance and were
soon being exported to many countries; Mrs. I. Earnshaw's 'Heather-
pines' were doing well; Mrs. C. Roberts showed her 'Petrozanne'
cats' and Mrs. D. Winsor's 'Tranby' stock was becoming well-
known. Cats bearing the 'Contented' prefix of Miss I. Wiseman
began to appear among the winners, as did the 'Colewoods' bred by
Miss M. E. Smith (with 'Colaswood' prefix), the 'Selbornes' of Mrs. M.
Foxwell and the 'Hillcross' cats of Mrs. E. Towe, to mention just a
few. The numbers have increased slowly over the years, there being
nearly 100 in the last stud book published by the Governing Council
of the Cat Fancy in 1969, but far more are registered than that. Con-
sistently among the recent winners, in addition to those already
mentioned, are the 'Amharics' of Mrs. M. Knight, the 'Berninas' of
Mrs. D. Threadingham, the 'Abyseals' of Mrs. L. Bradbury, the
'Courtmoors' of Mrs. Burrows, and the 'Shybus' of Mrs. S. Bullock.
These are only a few picked out at random from a long list.   45

As previously stated, the usual fur colouring of the Abyssinian is a rich rufous red, but over the years kittens with dark grey or silver coats have been known, and as long ago as 1887 a kitten with a red coat is said to have been born in a litter, but what happened to it is not known. Other red kittens appeared from time to time, but it was not always realised that they were from pure breeding and often the poor female was accused, quite wrongly, of having mismated. The original Abyssinians (referred to as 'Ruddy' in the United States and Canada) have ruddy-brown fur, with each hair having two or three darker-coloured bands, but those kittens that cropped up occasionally had coats that were rich copper red in colour, with darker double or treble ticking. Although born in the same litter as the original, which are Breed No. 23, the few red kittens that arrived had to be registered as 'Any other Variety' and could not compete in the Abyssinian open classes at the shows. Naturally, the breeders were annoyed about this, especially as it was eventually realised that these kittens appeared only from certain strains, and it soon became obvious that for reds to be produced it was necessary for both parents to carry the gene. Far from being 'Any other variety', it was agreed that such kittens were entirely pure bred, and in due course in 1963 Reds were granted a breed number (23a) as a separate variety and were thus qualified to have their own open class at the shows and become Champions in due course.

Over the years several breeders had been interested in producing the Reds, and the late Mrs. V. Major had one unexpectedly in a litter in the early 1950s which was bought by the late Mrs. D. Winsor. However, as there was no suitable male as a mate for her at that time she failed to produce any red kittens, as she unfortunately died at an early age. Other fanciers, such as Mrs. M. Eustace, the well-known writer and cat judge, had one of the early ones, and Lady Liverpool too became interested in Reds. A red kitten of her breeding was sold to Mrs. Winsor. One strain of Mrs. E. Menezes' 'Taishun' Abyssinians proved to carry the red gene and she was able to let Mrs. D. Winsor have a beautiful red male kitten 'Taishun Khephra', and red Abyssinian kittens sired by him were soon being exported all over the world.

It is not necessary for the parents to be red to produce kittens of that colour; only for both to carry the gene. An excellent example of this is Miss H. Scatchard's 'Ch. Philos Precious Topaz', a beautiful red female, whose father is Ch. Taishun Leo and whose mother is Abyseal Jade, both having normal colouring. Mrs. D. Threadingham has several red champions bearing her Bernina prefix with red on

46

both sides, and Mrs. M. Macalister has a red, Kuala Amber Arusi, from this breeding.

In addition to the normal, referred to as Ruddy in the United States and Canada, and the Red, it has been found possible to produce Abyssinians with coats of differing colours. That Silver was possible has been known for many years, and Lady Barnard was said to have bred some Albinos, but not at shows. Blues have been seen and one in particular, Fairlee Mehesso, a male bred by Mrs. Evely, has attracted much attention. Cream and Lilacs have also been bred. These colour variations are not yet officially recognised and are, therefore, registered as 'Any Other Variety'.

The Abyssinian Cat Club, whose secretary is Mrs. I. Earnshaw, Heatherpine, Curridge, Newbury, Berkshire, looks after the interests of the Abyssinians.

Abyssinian. Ch. Taishum Sabina with Kitten. Owned by Mrs. Menezes
Photographer Anne Cumbers

STANDARD OF POINTS

ABYSSINIAN—BREED 23

Colour and Type: Ruddy brown, ticked with black or dark brown, double or treble ticking, i.e. two or three bands of colour on each hair preferable to single ticking; no bars or other markings except that a dark spine line will not count against an otherwise good specimen. Inside of forelegs and belly should be of a tint to harmonise well with the main colour, the preference being given to orange-brown.

Absence of Markings: i.e. bars on head, tail, face and chest – is a very important property in this breed. These places are just where, if a cat or other feline animal shows markings at all, they will hold their ground to the last with remarkable obstinacy. The less markings visible the better; at the same time, the judge must not attach such undue importance to this property that he fails to give due importance to others. For instance, it does not follow that an absolutely unmarked cat, but of cobby build, failing in ticking and colour, is, because of absence of marking, better than a cat of slender build, well ticked and of nice colour, but handicapped by a certain amount of barring on legs and tail.

Head and Ears: Head, long and pointed, ears sharp, comparatively large and broad at base.

Eyes: large, bright and expressive. Colour: Green, yellow or hazel.

Tail: Fairly long and tapering.

Feet: Small, pads black, this colour also extending up the back of the hind legs.

Coat: Short, fine and close.

Size: Never large or coarse.

SCALE OF POINTS

Colour:	Body colour ..	..	..	30
	Ticking	..	..	20
Type:	Head and ears	..	..	15
	Eyes	..	..	5
	Body shape, tail, feet, coat			
	and carriage	..	..	20
	General condition	..	..	10
				100

NOTE. Although imperfect cats may be awarded prizes according to the merit of the entry, no Abyssinian should be awarded a champion certificate if it has distinct bars and rings on legs and tail; white chin to be considered undesirable; other white markings not permissible.

RED ABYSSINIAN—BREED 23a

The Red Abyssinian is the same in every respect as the Standard Abyssinian, except for colour, which is as follows:—

The body colour is rich copper red, doubly, or preferably trebly, ticked with darker colours. Lack of distinct contrast in the tickings is a fault. The richer the body colour the better. A pale colour is a bad fault.

The belly and inside of legs should be deep apricot to harmonise. The tail tip is dark brown and this may extend along the tail as a line. A spine line of deeper colour is permissible. The nose-leather is pink. Pads are pink, set in brown fur which extends up the back of the legs. Eye colours are as for Standard Abyssinians.

NOTE. As with the Standard Abyssinian, a white chin is to be considered undesirable, other white markings are not permissible.

Red Abyssinian "Taishum Jacaranda". Owned and bred by Mrs. Menezes   *Photographer Anne Cumbers*

7 Character and Personality of the Abyssinian

The very nature of the Abyssinians makes them ideal pets. They dislike close confinement and adore their freedom. If a male is kept for stud, it is essential that he be given as large a run as possible, and also, if at all possible, be allowed out in the garden under supervision for further exercise. Intensely active cats, they need to be able to run and play. Gentle and affectionate, they love to be noticed and frequently at the shows can be seen doing all they can to attract the attention of passers-by.

Ideal companions, especially for lonely people, they love company, being almost excessively friendly. Like the Siamese, they dislike spending long hours on their own, but, unlike many Siamese, they are not noisy cats, being very quiet of voice. Even when the females are in season it is sometimes difficult to know when they are calling, and many a breeder has been surprised to find her queen in kitten by a male of her choice, not even knowing that she had called. Because of this trait some breeders have found it better to keep a stud of their own, as the male will know before they do when the female is ready to mate.

They can easily be trained to walk on leads, and soon become used to travelling in a car, but like all cats they should never be allowed complete freedom in the car. Before now, their attempts to jump on their owners' shoulders or laps when driving have caused accidents.

When first born the kittens may have various dark markings which fade as the fur grows, but even shortly after birth the distinctive ruddy coat colour can easily be distinguished from that of the red. Many still have white chins, which are considered undesirable but have proved exceedingly difficult to breed out; white markings on the stomach and other places are considered very bad faults. Heavy markings around the neck, referred to as 'Lord Mayors' Chains', seldom fade and would be faulted by a judge if shown.

The kittens are sweet; adult cats in miniature, looking not unlike baby pumas with their tufted ears; very independent and like most of the other Foreign varieties, most forward in their development. When only three or four days old they may be crawling around the box, and at the age of 10 days or so they may try to climb out. Toilet training can start at the age of three weeks, and once shown where it is they will use it readily. They are happy kittens, 'trilling' rather than purring when playing or particularly pleased, and a joy to watch at play.

Like the Siamese, they are not great milk drinkers; indeed some cannot tolerate cows' milk at all and may suffer acute diarrhoea if given it. Some are able to take a little Carnation tinned milk, but all cats and kittens should always have access to plenty of clean drinking water. They are not fussy in their feeding, and usually do well on a good mixed diet with plenty of protein. Anyone buying a kitten should ask the breeder to supply a diet sheet, giving details of the feeding, and this should be strictly adhered to for the first week or two. Once the kitten has settled in, new items may be introduced a little at a time until the effect has been noted. The change from one home to another, even different drinking water, may result in constipation or loose motions, so it is essential, if possible, to keep the feeding much the same. If the kitten is constipated a little corn oil may be given, but if it is affected the other way the food should be given as dry as possible and all milk withheld. If the condition persists veterinary advice should be sought as soon as possible. If not already inoculated against Feline Infectious Enteritis this should be done once the kitten has settled in quite happily, and before it is allowed contact with other cats or allowed to run over ground frequented by them. A veterinary surgeon will advise about the correct age for the injection to be given.

Abyssinian kittens are in no way fragile and do not need excessive heat, but, like all kittens, should be kept away from draughts when young. In very cold weather a hot water bottle covered with a thick blanket is usually appreciated. They grow rapidly and eventually may be trained to do a few simple tricks. In fact, many teach themselves to beg like a dog, with paws waving in the air. They will readily retrieve small balls of paper thrown for them, and many love to sit with their paws around their owners' necks.

They make ideal pets for busy people, their fine short coats needing comparatively little grooming. Hard stroking with the hands will give the coats a good sheen. Some breeders prefer to use a brush with short hair bristles, others a rubber brush. Over-use of a comb with wide teeth is not advisable, as this tends to open up the fur and may also leave track marks. It is useful to have a narrow-toothed steel comb at hand for catching the occasional flea or removing loose hairs, dust and dirt from the coat. A few drops of bay rum sprinkled into the fur and a rubbing all over with a chamois leather is another

51

method favoured by some exhibitors to present their cats looking at their best at the shows. An Abyssinian may be a year or more old before the full beauty of the ticked adult coat is seen, and a male may be 18 months to two years old before he is old enough to use as a stud, but this does vary considerably. The age of maturity for the females also varies, some having their first season when only six or seven months old, others much later. The female should not be mated until at least 10 to 11 months of age and then not until her second call. The majority make excellent mothers, but occasionally one does resent being shut up with her kittens away from her owner and will stand at the door asking to come out. In this case a small kitten pen with the box in it is an asset, although it may be a nuisance, taking up a space in a kitchen or living room. But if the cat can be with her kittens and also see her owner it is frequently a happy solution.

The litters are not large, three to four being considered average, although seven is not unknown. For some reason, males always seem to predominate, so a litter with two of each sex is regarded as extremely good.

Most Abyssinians are sold as pets, and if not to be used for breeding it is advisable that they should be neutered. An Abyssinian neuter grows into a grand animal, most handsome in appearance; it matters little whether it is male or female, both being equally affectionate towards their owners, and making most decorative pets for many years to come.

Turkish Cat. "Kastamohou Yalali". Owner—Mrs. Tidmarsh
Photographer Anne Cumbers

8   History of the Turkish Cats and General Characteristics

HISTORY OF THE TURKISH CATS

The history of the domestic cat goes back several thousand years to the time of the Egyptians. It is usually surmised that the early cats were short-coated, but when and where those with the longer fur originated is still a matter of conjecture and much speculation. They were not seen in Europe until the 16th century when travellers brought back these different and unusual-looking cats from Ankara (then Angora—hence the name) in Turkey. There is evidence that they had been known and were much prized there for a very long time before this, probably originating in the first place through a mutation. They appear to have come to Britain via France and for a time were referred to as the French cats. When interest was shown in cat-breeding, and fanciers began to think of different types of cats, they were spoken of collectively as the Foreign or Eastern cats.

These cats with their long silky fur were considered very valuable and were much sought after, being few and far between. Harrison Weir said of them in his *Our Cats and All About Them* (Tunbridge Wells, 1889) that the Angora cats were great favourites with the Turks and Armenians and that the best 'of high value' were the pure white, with blue eyes 'being thought the perfection of cats all other points being good, and its hearing by no means defective'.

Their heads were small, or the noses shorter than those of the resident short-coated cats, and the ears were on the large size. Many of the Whites suffered from deafness, but this was not always realised by their owners, and they were often thought, quite wrongly, to be unresponsive and slow to learn. Cats with long coats were also introduced from Persia, but their heads were rounder, the noses shorter and the ears smaller. From Russia too came cats with long coats, usually with tabby markings. Their eyes were said to be round and orange in colour. The coat textures of these three varieties differed, as did the tail length, and Harrison Weir, when setting out his Points of Excellence for the first judging of cats at shows, made quite clear distinctions between the quality of the fur and the tail length of the Angoras, the Persians and the Russians.

Of these various cats, the look of those from Persia came to be preferred, and so the early fanciers managed by careful cross-breeding to produce cats with long silky coats, broad round heads, small ears, big round orange eyes, full ruffs and short tails. Gradually cats bearing any resemblance to the early ones from Turkey disappeared, and any that did appear at the shows were said to be old-fashioned and having bad type, and were not used for breeding. By the beginning of the 20th Century they appeared to be quite unknown; so much so that a noted breeder wrote that 'she had never been able to obtain any definite information as to the difference between the Persian and Angora cats'.

It was some 50 years later that Miss Laura Lushington and Miss Sonia Halliday, while travelling near the great lake in the Van area of Turkey, saw to their amazement a cat with true Angora type and a long silky white coat, but differing from the early cats that had come to Europe from Turkey in having deep auburn markings on the face and rings of the same colour on the tail. They made inquiries and found that such cats were a known breed in the area being mostly privately owned and much prized, and had a reputation for liking to swim in warm shallow pools and stream. Intrigued by this and the strong resemblance to the original long-hairs, they searched and managed to find an unrelated pair which they brought back to England. Later they went back several times and were able to find

54

Turkish Kitten. Bred by Mrs. Russell   *Photographer Anne Cumbers*

and bring back other unrelated cats with the same colourings. On
their release, after being in quarantine for six months, the cats were
mated and the resultant kittens looked exactly like their parents and
it was obvious that they were not a man-made breed, but were the
result of natural selection, probably through inter-breeding in an
isolated area.

No records had been kept in Turkey, so naturally these cats had
no pedigrees, and as the Governing Council insists on proof of pure
breeding for at least four generations and it was not possible to
obtain this, Miss Lushington had to register them as 'Any Other
Variety'. The first Turkish cats in Britain were given such names as
'Antalya Anatolia', 'Stambul Byzantium' and 'Burdor', and when in
1969 the prefix 'Van' was approved kittens appeared bearing such
exotic names as 'Van Kehrirar Iskenderun', 'Van Attla Stambul' and
'Van Antolia'. At first they appeared on exhibition only at the shows,
attracting a great deal of attention, and being frequently referred to
both in the press and on television as 'the swimming cats'. Most
cats will swim if forced to do so, but apparently these do so of their
own free will and have been seen doing so on television.

For several years both cats and kittens were entered and frequently won in the 'Any other variety' classes at the shows. More breeders became interested, and although there had never been any question that they were anything but pure bred pedigrees were gradually built up and before long there was definite proof of pure breeding going back for the required number of generations. In 1969, thanks to the efforts of the Colourpoint, Rex coated and A.O.V. Club, the Turkish cats were granted recognition, were given a breed number, and their standard was approved. They had their own open breed classes at the show and were able to compete for challenge certificates.

When the first kittens were born, as there were so few of them, Miss Lushington very wisely sold them only as neutered pets, to ensure that there would not be close inter-breeding. In the early stages of developing any new variety, or in this case when endeavouring to establish a very old one, it is important that the breeding be carried on to a set plan and that the mating of mother to son or father and daughter, frequently necessary when numbers are few, should not be done indiscriminately, as if done without pre-knowledge it is easy to duplicate faults instead of breeding them out, thus spoiling the whole programme. Such careful supervision has ensured that the

Turkish Van Bayan. Owner—Miss Lushington
Photographer Sonia Halliday

Turkish have always been bred close to the now-accepted standard. The importation of stock from Turkey from time to time has introduced new blood but still kept them pure, with no cross-breeding with other varieties.

After being granted recognition kittens appeared in a class of their own at the Kensington Kitten and Neuter Cat Club Show in 1969, and both cats and kittens now appear regularly at shows in their own classes. Several have won challenge certificates and by the time this book goes to press there will doubtless be several champions.

Among the Turkish cats now appearing at the shows as well as many bearing the Van prefix of Miss L. Lushington, there are some very good specimens, such as Miss S. Halliday's Tatvan Halide, Mr. H. Martin's Gelidonya kittens, Mrs. L. Russell's Kastamouhou Yalail, and Mrs. O. Jarman's Sirvan kittens. Mrs. A. Tidmarsh has acquired a number of the Van cats and before long her Vandaha kittens will be making their appearance and helping to increase still further the interest now shown in these delightful cats.

Not only in Britain but also in the United States has the wheel turned full circle, with cats bearing the original long-haired type taking their place once again in the cat world. In 1958 a Colonel Grant and his wife were also intrigued to see at the airport at Ankara a long-haired white cat with the 'old-fashioned' type. They discovered that the Zoo in Ankara had established a small cattery to breed these cats, as they appeared to be in danger of extinction. Their coats were pure white with no markings. The eyes were usually blue or one eye was blue and the other amber, as in the original cats of several hundred years ago. The Grants were fascinated by this and when they returned to the United States in 1962 'Yildiz' and 'Yildizcik' went with them. This pair had kittens, but carrying out the same strict policy as Miss L. Lushington had in Britain the kittens were all sold as pets on the understanding that they would be neutered and not used for breeding. Other cats were obtained from the Ankara Zoo, and kittens that could be bred from were sold only to selected breeders dedicated to keeping the variety pure.

The kittens were all white, with eyes of blue, or odd eyes, or amber eyes. Although some of those with blue eyes were deaf the percentage was not as great as had been anticipated.

In 1968 the Cat Fanciers' Association Inc. agreed that they could be registered as 'Angoras', and in 1970 they were officially recognised as a breed for show purposes and granted a provisional standard. A number of fanciers are breeding them in the States and there are probably far more there now than in Turkey, the country of origin 57 of the original long-haired cats so long ago. As there is no quarantine in to the United States for cats from Britain it is possible that before long the 'Turkish' ones will be seen there. The strict quarantine law in Britain that any cat entering the country must be kept in an approved quarantine cattery for six months makes the importation of any cat or kitten a very expensive business and as yet no 'Angora' cat has been seen.

Turkish Cat "Van Fethiye". Owner—Mrs. L. Russell. Breeder—Miss L. Lushington   *Photographer Anne Cumbers*

9 Character and Personality of the Turkish Cats

In the Van area in Turkey, the Turkish cats, known there as the Van cats, have the reputation of liking to swim in warm shallow streams and rivers. It is a fallacy to say all cats hate water, for most will swim if forced to do so, but apparently this variety in Turkey does so of its own free will. It is unwise, however, to encourage them to swim in rivers and ponds in Britain, because the water temperature here can be very cold, and some cats are prone to catching colds. They do love to play with water, and will sit in the sink patting at the drips from the taps.

So far the litters born in Britain seem to average about four in number, with the males and females appearing in fairly equal numbers. When born, although so tiny, they are like small adults in miniature. Unlike most newly-born white kittens, they do not have the usual pink appearance, but have the chalk-white coats and the distinctive auburn markings showing up quite clearly.

The long straight fur grows quite rapidly, but as there is no thick undercoat to fluff it up it never obtains the full appearance of the coats of the Longhairs produced here by selective breeding. The texture is beautiful to feel, being extremely silky, with the pure chalk-white colouring making a wonderful contrast with the bright auburn markings on the face. Ideally, these markings should be on the face below and around the ears, leaving a white blaze between the markings going over the head, with the nose, cheeks and lower part of the face pure white. Sometimes, too, auburn markings which are not called for in the standard appear on the body, but if a cat is outstanding in every other respect it should not be penalised too severely for these when being judged.

It is strange, and is probably due to the climate in their country of origin, but in the summer they tend to shed their fur far more than most other long-haired cats, looking fairly short-coated, but as the cold weather approaches the fur grows rapidly, becoming far more luxurious.

The head shape differs from the other long-hairs, being a little longer and having a short wedge-shaped muzzle; the well-feathered   59 ears, too, are larger and more upright, and the nose is definitely long, not at all snub. The round lustrous eyes are pale amber, and pink-rimmed, with the nose leather and the pads to the paws also a delicate shade of pink.

The body is long and sturdy, on medium-length legs on smallish paws, and full tail should be of medium length, auburn in colour and ringed in a deeper shade of the same colour. The males are noticeably of heavier build around the neck and shoulders.

The rate of growth and progress from kittenhood is strangely like that of the Foreign shorthairs rather than that of the longhairs; the eyes opening when the kittens are about four to five days old; climbing out of the box when only two weeks old, perhaps patting at one another at three weeks, and really playing together when four or five weeks old. Like all kittens, the eyes are bright blue when born, the amber colouring coming through gradually.

Some of the early Turkish cats appeared to be of nervous disposition and rather shy of people, but it has been found that if they are brought up in the house and handled from an early age, so becoming used to people, the kittens show no signs of nervousness and are full of fun and become most affectionate.

They are easy cats to groom, for if their long silky coats are attended to daily, if only for a few minutes, they rarely knot up as does the fur of many of the other longhairs.

It is most important to groom correctly, as over-harsh grooming may harm the soft silky fur. A wide-toothed steel comb, and one with fine teeth for removing any dirt and possibly the occasional flea are really all that is needed. The use of a brush is not recommended as brushing makes the hair too springy and flyaway. If, however, there are bad greasy patches caused by constant stroking a little talcum powder may be sprinkled well in and then brushed out gently with a soft brush with hair bristles. But over use of the brush must be avoided.

During the grooming period the ears and the corners of the eyes should be examined to make sure they are not dirty, any dust being wiped away with a little dampened cotton wool. The Turkish cats rarely suffer from running eyes due to overtyping, with the brownish matter causing furrows each side of the nose as happens to some longhairs, as their noses are not nearly so flat and short. In fact, if the noses are snub, it would be considered a definite fault if being exhibited.

Most breeders and exhibitors of this variety advocate bathing a day or two before the show, using a baby shampoo. Nothing harsher

Turkish Cat "Gelidanya Karides" with kitten. Owner—Mrs. Russell
Photographer Anne Cumbers

should be used as it could spoil the silkiness of the fur. As they like water they seem to enjoy their bath more than most cats. The ears should be plugged with cotton wool before the cat is stood in an inch or two of warm water in the kitchen sink, which is a nice height for handling. Never use water that is too hot. The fur should be wetted all over, and the shampoo sprinkled on and rubbed into the fur, taking care to avoid the eyes. It should be rinsed out completely, with a hand spray if possible. This should be repeated, and the rinsing continued until all traces of the shampoo have gone. The coat should be gently rubbed dry with a soft towel, or dried with a hand dryer, if the cat does not object. The pink padded paws should be examined to ensure that they are quite clean and the tail, especially that of the male, washed carefully to make sure it is free of any yellow staining.

61

The cat should be kept away from draughts and not allowed out until the coat is completely dry. Until the day of the show care will have to be taken to keep the cat as clean as possible, and the coat lightly combed only.

Any kittens not to be used for breeding should be neutered, particularly the males, as if the variety is to be kept pure they should not be used as studs for any other variety and since there are as yet comparatively few breeding queens about they will not get enough work to keep them happy. Females, too, should be spayed if not required for breeding. If it is desired that they should have kittens arrangements should be made well in advance with the owner of the nearest Turkish stud, and never with a stud of another variety. A female should never be overbred from, one litter a year being sufficient, two at the utmost. They usually make very good mothers, really loving their kittens, keeping them beautifully white.

Turkish "Van Bayan". Owned and bred by Miss Lushington
Photographer Sonia Halliday

A full-grown neutered Turkish cat is a delightful pet to have about the house, certainly most distinctive and unusual too in appearance, and also because the oldest long-haired variety that had almost vanished is once again being seen as 'the pet in the drawing room'.

As a postscript to this chapter it should be mentioned here that their general care and attention is much the same as for other cats, but in feeding the majority seem to prefer raw meat to anything, and clean water to drink.

STANDARD OF POINTS

Colour and Coat: The colour should be chalk white with no trace of yellow. Auburn markings on face with white blaze. Ears should be white; nose tip, pads and inside ears should be a delicate shell pink. Fur should be long, soft and silky to the roots. No woolly undercoat.

Head: Short wedge; well feathered large ears upright and set fairly close together; long nose.

Eyes: Shape should be round, colour should be light amber, rims should be pink skinned.

Body: Long but sturdy, legs medium in length; neat round feet with well tufted toes. Males should be particularly muscular on neck and shoulders.

Brush: Full, medium length, auburn in colour with faint auburn rings in cats, more distinct ring markings in kittens.

Scale of points					
Colour and Coat	..	..	..		35
Head	..	..	..	..	25
Eyes	..	..	..	..	10
Body	..	..	..	..	10
Brush	..	..	..	..	10
Condition	..	..	..	..	10
					100

NOTE. This is the ideal; occasionally some cats may have small auburn markings irregularly placed, but this should not disqualify an otherwise good specimen.

10 Buying a Kitten

Because Rex, Abyssinian and Turkish cats are still rare, it will probably be difficult to find one. As in all cases where the future owner wants to buy a pedigree kitten, it is wise to visit a well-known breeder, see the various types of cats and the way they are kept, and then to book a kitten.

There are still long waiting lists for these kittens, so it may be some months before one can be bought. We always tell prospective owners when the litter arrives and then the kittens can be visited when quite young, and their fascinating progress can be watched.

The Secretaries of the Specialist Clubs have lists of reputable breeders (the Secretaries' addresses can be found in the appropriate chapter).

When the kitten is booked it is time to buy the few articles that are necessary to welcome the new member of the family. For it must be stressed that these kittens will demand to be a member of the family. Abyssinian, Rex and Turkish, like most cats, do not take happily to being kept in one room and appreciated for their decorative value only. They will demand, and give, affection and will want to know exactly what is happening in the household. Rex cats, like Turkish, love water and will balance on the sides of the bath at bathtime, and they adore sharing a telephone call.

The first necessity for a new kitten is a basket, preferably one with a 'hood' to keep out draughts, but a cardboard box with a warm blanket makes a good substitute. Sharing master's bed is first favourite, but a basket is second best. The warm blanket should be easy to wash.

A sanitary-tray is essential, for even if a kitten has access to a garden, for the first weeks he must be kept indoors and so will need his own tray. Very reasonably-priced plastic trays which are easily washable can be obtained at any branch of Boots: and for a longer-lasting and better-looking tray, one can be bought by mail from The Cat's Accessories, 1, Newnham Street, Bedford. Where there is only one cat in the household the ideal material to use in a sanitary-tray is one of the proprietary makes of cat litter. However, this can be rather expensive and cheaper materials are peat, sand or

Abyssinian Kittens, 3 weeks old. Owned and bred by Mrs. Menezes
(Taishun prefix)   *Photographer Anne Cumbers*

wood-chips. Sawdust is not advisable, as it tends to get into a kitten's
mouth and nostrils. Naturally, if a garden is available it is as well,
after the kitten has had time to become used to its new home, to
train it to go out there – at first under supervision, and later on its
own.

As well as a plastic bowl and two plastic feeding-dishes, a
kitten should have a natural bristle brush for grooming and a flea-
comb, for even the healthiest kitten may harbour these parasites.

Then the exciting day comes for the kitten to be collected. It is
still advisable to examine the kitten carefully. His eyes should be
clean and bright –any pink rim or 'crustiness' is a sign that he may
have been suffering from conjunctivitis which can be difficult to clear.

His ears should be clean, even deep inside the many little crevices.
Any wax that there may be should be honey-coloured. A *dark-
coloured* wax or discharge is a sign of canker, usually caused by
ear-mite.

The coat should be clean, soft and glossy. A harsh or 'open' coat is a sign that the kitten is not well, as also is any offensive discharge from the anus. The kitten should feel heavy, even when small. A 'light-as-air' kitten is adorable, but is often frail because of some illness or hereditary defect. The coat should also be free from fleas. These cannot always be seen, but flea-dirt, looking like tiny specks of black dust, is found lying between the hairs and is a sure sign that livestock is present.

A healthy kitten will always appear alert and lively. We always prefer a kitten that has been reared in the house, for one brought up in an outdoor run, away from the bustle of a household, always tends to be nervous. This nervousness can usually be overcome in time, but the owner needs extra patience.

Any reputable breeder will supply a diet sheet with any kitten that is sold, as a sudden change in diet can cause quite severe tummy-upsets. A kitten's diet should be as varied as possible, and should contain the basic proteins, fats, carbohydrates, vitamins and minerals. Though the modern tinned foods are good, tinned food alone can never be sufficient, even though they are 'vitamin-enriched'.

Every kitten's needs and likes may vary *slightly*, but the following diet is one generally acceptable and includes all that is necessary, although raw liver can cause loose motions in some kittens:

7.30 a.m. 1 teaspoon Farex mixed to a thin cream with warm diluted Carnation milk and $\frac{1}{4}$ teaspoon glucose.

12 a.m. $1\frac{1}{2}$ tablespoons fine-chopped raw beef or liver mixed with a little puppy meal and stock or gravy (to this add 1 teaspoon shredded suet for Rex kittens as this supplies the extra fat so necessary for the Rex coat).

4.30 p.m. $1\frac{1}{2}$ tablespoons cooked rabbit, fish or chicken, or 1 heaped tablespoon 'Chum', 'Paws' or 'Spratts' meat mixed with a little puppy-meal or cornflakes.

7.30 p.m. Farex as at 7.30 a.m. can be alternated with a well-beaten egg, which most kittens love.

Some breeders use cows' milk instead of Carnation milk, but it can cause diarrhoea in some kittens due to its high percentage of lactose.

In addition to this, a supply of fresh water should always be available. Four tablets of 'Kit-zyme' daily are a valuable conditioner. These mineral-enriched yeast tablets are much enjoyed by most cats, who crunch them as 'sweets'.

66 If the kitten is a poor eater or if it is at all out of condition it is

advisable to give a vitamin supplement. Many veterinary surgeons advise Vitavel, a pleasant orange-flavoured syrup that most cats seem to like. Half a teaspoonful, mixed with the 4.30 p.m. feed, supplies adequate vitamins.

The quantities given are suitable for an eight- to ten-week-old kitten. As the kitten grows the amounts should be slightly increased, and the Farex-milk omitted, until at six months the kitten is getting $\frac{3}{4}$ oz. per pound of body-weight. This amount should remain constant throughout the cat's adult life. An over-fat cat is never healthy. Nutritionists advocate $\frac{1}{2}$ oz. per pound of body-weight for ordinary cats, but with Rex cats there is a greater loss of body-heat due to their lack of coat-layers, and their need for food is greater. Of course, when a cat is pregnant the diet will need adjustment, but this is dealt with in a later chapter.

The new owner should ask the breeder if the kitten has been wormed. A vermifuge is normally given to the mother immediately after mating and again a fortnight later. The two doses are essential as the drug—usually Piperazine—kills only the developed worms,

Belgian Abyssinian. Owner—Madame Gethmann
Photographer FOTO FOCAT. Rotterdam

and does not affect the larvae. Since the life-cycle of a larva is two weeks before it hatches into a worm, the necessity for the two doses is obvious. If the mother has been kept worm-free in this way, and her nipples are carefully washed before the birth of her kittens, worming the kittens may not be necessary. Signs of worms (which are almost always roundworms) are an open or 'staring' coat, thinness and a poor or ravenous appetite. It is always wise to consult the veterinary surgeon before worming kittens, as he will advise the correct age for worming and also the correct dosage.

The administration of Piperazine is very different to the rather dangerous vermifuges used a few years ago. The dose is usually given after the morning feed, and followed with a teaspoon of milk of magnesia an hour later. This ensures that there is a bowel-action within three hours. Even if the kitten has worms it is quite usual not to see any traces in the motion, even though the dose has been effective.

One extremely important point when buying a kitten is to discover if it has been inoculated against the dreaded Feline Infectious Enteritis (Panleucopaenia). This is a highly-infectious and contagious disease, transmitted from cats and their human contacts and even from infected ground or articles. The disease is usually fatal in cats and almost certainly in young kittens.

The *only* safeguard is by inoculation with a vaccine at the age of six to ten weeks. There are several reliable makes of vaccine and any veterinary surgeon who is used to dealing with cats will recommend the vaccine that he has found best. Two injections of vaccine, at a fortnight's interval, are necessary with most vaccines, but the new 'Katavac' is given in one dose at 10 weeks. Immunisation is not complete until 10 days after the final dose, so the kitten should not be allowed out until he is fully immunised. If this has not been done by the breeder the new owner must have it done immediately.

Most veterinary surgeons advise that the inoculation be 'boosted' yearly for cats in a cattery, or for those which are show cats. For the pet living quietly at home it is probably not necessary.

Because of their rarity, prices of these kittens remain high, but the prices *should* include both inoculation and registration with the G.C.C.F. We have estimated that it costs us £14 to rear a kitten to the age of three months, and we consider ourselves fortunate if we cover our costs by the sales of kittens.

However, the joy of watching a healthy kitten at play cannot be measured in terms of cash, and the companionship they give is equal to that of most human friends.

Watermill Kandy Floss (Dam) with Britain's first White Cornish Rex Kittens and plain coated sisters. Owned and bred by Mrs. Ashford *Photographer Anne Cumbers*

11 The Brood Queen and Breeding

An increasing number of people are becoming interested in breeding pedigree cats, and among these people many choose the newer breeds, because of their unusual beauty and their reputation for being good 'breeders'.

There can be few more satisfying and heart-warming sights than a mother cat safely tucked up with her new kittens. Recently a psychiatrist gave his opinion that the caring-for and breeding of cats and dogs was in itself a form of psychotherapy. Certainly, in the care of breeding stock the problems of every-day living tend to get overlooked in the joy of helping to bring healthy new lives into being.

It should be stressed that cat-breeding can *never* be a purely profitable 'business' and if anyone thinks of taking it up with ideas of financial gain, they had better think of something else. If all goes well, the kittens are born normally and by the age of 10 weeks can be inoculated and sold. But the cost of heating, feeding and inoculation will take at least half of the 'profits' of selling the kittens. The remaining 'profit' will be needed for the extra food for the queen, her stud fee, and any additional medicines, such as vermifuges, vitamins and flea powders.

However, if the cat-owner is satisfied with the non-material profits, these are innumerable. The great drawback is that one usually wants to keep all the kittens, for each one has its own lovable character.

In choosing a female kitten or 'queen' for future breeding, the main points to look for are, of course, an abundance of health, and a pedigree that is not too in-bred. In a new breed, there is certain to be some in-breeding, and this has not proved detrimental to these lovely cats. However, repeated brother-to-sister matings (the closest of all relations) should be avoided. With Rex cats, the queen should also have a good, even, coat, for it is this attribute which is being aimed at by responsible Rex breeders.

A queen will normally have her first season or 'call' when she is about seven months old, though a few precocious kittens may call for the first time at five months. A first call may easily pass unnoticed, for these cats are not very vocal and the only signs may be that the queen is exceptionally affectionate, and spends her time rubbing round the furniture or her owner's legs.

But the local tom-cats will know the minute she starts to call and will be ready to rape her if they have the chance. So as soon as she shows any signs she must be kept indoors under lock and key.

The ideal time to mate a queen is at 10 months. By then she is fully-grown, but is still very young and supple and will give birth very easily. If she does not call until she is 10 months old she should not be mated until her second call, as so often the first call is a half-hearted affair. On the other hand, no queen should be allowed to call for more than three seasons without being mated, as if she is persistently 'held back' she may develop a neurosis and there is also the possibility that she may develop ovarian cysts. Even if she does not become neurotic, her owner may well do so, as a frustrated queen is wearing on the nerves!

At the queen's first call her owner should give careful thought as to who her mate should be. The G.C.C.F. issue an annual list of cats at stud; there may be an advertisement in *Fur and Feather*; club secretaries may be able to supply names and addresses; but for these comparatively rare varieties there is not much choice of stud. Fellow breeders may help, as not all advertise their males at public stud, but may be willing to take one or two females. Never send a maiden queen to an inexperienced male. Obviously the stud must be

Annelida Curly Coon, Cornish Rex with her 1 week old kittens. Owned and bred by Mrs. A. Ashford

Photographer Anne Cumbers

of the same genotype, and should, if possible, excel in any points in which the queen is lacking.

Having chosen a possible stud, it is very important that the queen's owner visits the stud's quarters. Even today very lovely stud-cats are kept in really terrible conditions, and a queen visiting such a stud runs a very great risk of contracting a possibly fatal

71

illness, not to mention a whole host of fleas and ear-mites! Any reputable stud owner will be pleased to show her stud and his quarters to owners of a queen, and if all is satisfactory, and both stud's and queen's pedigrees are mutually approved, a tentative booking can be made. Then, as soon as the queen's season comes round again (the time between seasons is usually 3—4 weeks) her owner needs only to phone the stud owner to check if he is free to receive her queen.

If possible the queen should be taken personally to the stud, as a long journey alone will sometimes frighten the queen, and she may be almost 'off call' by the time she arrives. However, if a personal escort is impossible she should be comfortably tucked up in a large travelling-basket, the sides of which should be covered with brown paper to keep out draughts. The basket should be clearly labelled with the stud owner's name. 'To be called for at .... station' should be written in large letters, and the stud owner should be notified of the exact time of the train's arrival. We have safely received queens from Scotland and Wales in this way, and they have been none the worse for their long journey.

It is usual for a queen to remain with the stud for about three days. She will not, of course, be with him all the time. She should be kept in a separate pen and allowed with the stud only during the actual mating. A 'maiden' queen may resent the male's advances for the first day or so. An experienced stud owner will not, however, be discouraged, but will try the queen with the stud at frequent intervals, arousing her first by stroking her along the back and around the tail. It is extremely unusual for a queen to completely refuse to mate, though it does happen very occasionally. It is usual to give a queen at least two or three matings with the stud.

Once the queen has returned home from stud she should be allowed to live her usual routine. The period of gestation is from 63—66 days, the most usual day of kittening being on the 65th day. (See table of gestation dates, pp 74-75.) The first signs of pregnancy can sometimes be detected exactly 21 days after the mating, when the nipples will start to show a deeper pink and will gradually increase in size. The queen herself will probably not show any change in her figure until after the fifth week of pregnancy.

If the queen fails to conceive from the first matings a stud owner will usually give her a free second stud service. The queen-owner should realise that this is only an act of courtesy and that a free service cannot be demanded. With the present high cost of food it is also expected that a queen's owner should pay for the queen's keep on her second visit.

Very occasionally a queen will persistently fail to conceive. A few years ago breeders would have written her off as a hopeless breeder. But with the advances made in veterinary science there is now a solution to the problem. It is known that cats (unlike humans who ovulate regularly once very month) ovulate only at *the time of mating.* A very few queens are lacking in essential hormones and fail to ovulate at mating, and therefore fail to conceive. In cases like this veterinary surgeons advise that the queen be given an injection of luteinising hormone shortly after the first mating, a couple of hours before the second mating. This injection causes ovulation to occur and the queen then conceives normally. This injection has been a god-send to 'difficult' queens. It is not a cheap treatment, but very worthwhile if it results in a litter of bonny kittens!

At about the fifth week after mating the queen's diet should be

Two Sherada Kittens, Brown Abyssinians. Dam: Ch. Flume Atalanta. Sire: Ch. Shybu Koralai. Owned and bred by Mr. and Mrs. Warde   *Photographer Mike Randall*

BREEDING TABLE

January

Mated	1	2	3	4	5	6	7	8	9	10	11	12	13	14	15	16
Kittens	7	8	9	10	11	12	13	14	15	16	17	18	19	20	21	22

March

January

Mated	17	18	19	20	21	22	23	24	25	26	27	28	29	30	31
Kittens	23	24	25	26	27	28	29	30	31	1	2	3	4	5	6

March   April

February

Mated	1	2	3	4	5	6	7	8	9	10	11	12	13	14
Kittens	7	8	9	10	11	12	13	14	15	16	17	18	19	20

April

February

Mated	15	16	17	18	19	20	21	22	23	24	25	26	27	28
Kittens	21	22	23	24	25	26	27	28	29	30	1	2	3	4

April   May

March

Mated	1	2	3	4	5	6	7	8	9	10	11	12	13	14	15	16
Kittens	5	6	7	8	9	10	11	12	13	14	15	16	17	18	19	20

May

March

Mated	17	18	19	20	21	22	23	24	25	26	27	28	29	30	31
Kittens	21	22	23	24	25	26	27	28	29	30	31	1	2	3	4

May   June

April

Mated	1	2	3	4	5	6	7	8	9	10	11	12	13	14	15
Kittens	5	6	7	8	9	10	11	12	13	14	15	16	17	18	19

June

April

Mated	16	17	18	19	20	21	22	23	24	25	26	27	28	29	30
Kittens	20	21	22	23	24	25	26	27	28	29	30	1	2	3	4

June   July

May

Mated	1	2	3	4	5	6	7	8	9	10	11	12	13	14	15	16
Kittens	5	6	7	8	9	10	11	12	13	14	15	16	17	18	19	20

July

May

Mated	17	18	19	20	21	22	23	24	25	26	27	28	29	30	31
Kittens	21	22	23	24	25	26	27	28	29	30	31	1	2	3	4

July   August

June

Mated	1	2	3	4	5	6	7	8	9	10	11	12	13	14	15
Kittens	5	6	7	8	9	10	11	12	13	14	15	16	17	18	19

August

June

Mated	16	17	18	19	20	21	22	23	24	25	26	27	28	29	30
Kittens	20	21	22	23	24	25	26	27	28	29	30	31	1	2	3

August   September

The Brood Queen and Breeding

	July															
Mated	1	2	3	4	5	6	7	8	9	10	11	12	13	14	15	16
Kittens	4	5	6	7	8	9	10	11	12	13	14	15	16	17	18	19

September

	July														
Mated	17	18	19	20	21	22	23	24	25	26	27	28	29	30	31
Kittens	20	21	22	23	24	25	26	27	28	29	30	1	2	3	4

September   October

	August															
Mated	1	2	3	4	5	6	7	8	9	10	11	12	13	14	15	16
Kittens	5	6	7	8	9	10	11	12	13	14	15	16	17	18	19	20

October

	August														
Mated	17	18	19	20	21	22	23	24	25	26	27	28	29	30	31
Kittens	21	22	23	24	25	26	27	28	29	30	31	1	2	3	4

October   November

	September														
Mated	1	2	3	4	5	6	7	8	9	10	11	12	13	14	15
Kittens	5	6	7	8	9	10	11	12	13	14	15	16	17	18	19

November

	September														
Mated	16	17	18	19	20	21	22	23	24	25	26	27	28	29	30
Kittens	20	21	22	23	24	25	26	27	28	29	30	1	2	3	4

November   December

	October															
Mated	1	2	3	4	5	6	7	8	9	10	11	12	13	14	15	16
Kittens	5	6	7	8	9	10	11	12	13	14	15	16	17	18	19	20

December

	October														
Mated	17	18	19	20	21	22	23	24	25	26	27	28	29	30	31
Kittens	21	22	23	24	25	26	27	28	29	30	31	1	2	3	4

December   January

	November														
Mated	1	2	3	4	5	6	7	8	9	10	11	12	13	14	15
Kittens	5	6	7	8	9	10	11	12	13	14	15	16	17	18	19

January

	November														
Mated	16	17	18	19	20	21	22	23	24	25	26	27	28	29	30
Kittens	20	21	22	23	24	25	26	27	28	29	30	31	1	2	3

January   February

	December															
Mated	1	2	3	4	5	6	7	8	9	10	11	12	13	14	15	16
Kittens	4	5	6	7	8	9	10	11	12	13	14	15	16	17	18	19

February

	December														
Mated	17	18	19	20	21	22	23	24	25	26	27	28	29	30	31
Kittens	20	21	22	23	24	25	26	27	28	1	2	3	4	5	6

February   March

adjusted to include four small meat meals during the day and at least one of milk or evaporated milk. She should also be given additional minerals and calcium in the form of veterinary yeast; if recommended by the vet, one teaspoon of Crookes Collo-cal-D each day can also be given.

A fortnight before the kittens are due the queen should be introduced to her kittening-box. The ideal box for this is a tea-chest standing on its side. The 'roof' of this chest should be partially cut out, and suspended over it should be a Dull Emitter Infra-Red Lamp. These lamps are a life-saver for small or premature kittens and are also for the Rex essential during the winter months, and are appreciated by the Abyssinian and Turkish. Wrenn's of Willow Farm, Sheldon, Honiton, Devon, specialise in making these lamps for cats.

A narrow wooden rail should be fitted inside the chest, two inches from the floor of the chest and two inches from the sides (see diagram). This is to ensure that if the queen is restless during and after labour newborn kittens are not crushed by her against the sides of the box. This is a tip gleaned from pig-breeders!

The chest should be supplied with a couple of newspapers which the queen will happily tear up when preparing her 'nest'. She may decide that she prefers the airing-cupboard or even the larder, but she will eventually be persuaded to have her babies in the appointed place.

Novice breeders always worry that they will not know when labour starts. Early signs are that the queen becomes increasingly restless, following her owner about from room to room, and demanding extra affection. It is a wise plan to check the rectal temperature for three days prior to the date of kittening. When labour is imminent the queen's temperature will drop by approximately one degree.

As the first stages of labour start the queen will climb into her box. Some insist on having their owners by their side when kittening, but others produce their kittens before the owners are even aware that labour has started. It can be noticed that the rate of respiration is slightly increased during the early stages.

As contractions occur the queen can be seen to be straining. At first these contractions may only occur half-hourly, but as labour progresses they become more frequent, until the queen is straining roughly once a minute. There is no definite length of time during which the first stages will continue. If the queen is straining every

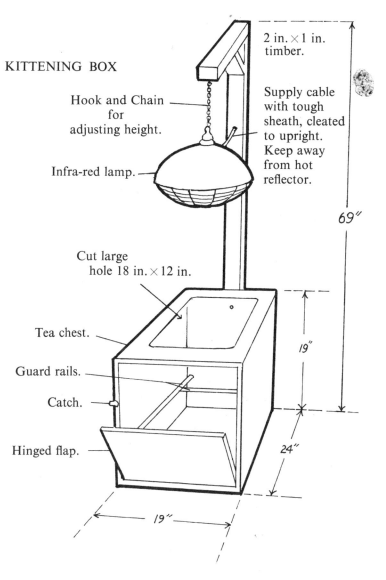

KITTENING BOX

2 in. × 1 in. timber.

Hook and Chain for adjusting height.

Supply cable with tough sheath, cleated to upright. Keep away from hot reflector.

Infra-red lamp.

69″

Cut large hole 18 in. × 12 in.

Tea chest.

19″

Guard rails.

Catch.

24″

Hinged flap.

19″

IMPORTANT. Use only cable with toughest possible sheathing because of cat's claws and teeth.

77

minute for longer than an hour the veterinary surgeon should be informed as there could be complications.

Normally, after about 20 to 30 minutes of frequent contractions, the amniotic sac (the 'envelope' enclosing the kitten and the amniotic fluid) can be seen protruding from the dilated vagina. At this point the queen will start to lick the vulva and may perforate the sac. It will still be some minutes, possibly even 20 minutes, before the kitten is finally expelled. As soon as it is born, the queen should lick it thoroughly to remove the sac and any remaining fluid, and to encourage the first breaths. She will probably not attempt to bite the cord till the placenta (afterbirth) is expelled, possibly several minutes after the birth of each kitten. If the queen ignores the new-born kitten completely for more than four minutes the owner must then take action if the kitten's life is to be saved. The majority of cats are exceptionally good with their kittens and it is very seldom that any human help is needed.

However, if the mother ignores the kitten the owner should clean the face gently with a towel and gradually peel off the remaining sac. The cord must then be severed at *least* three inches from the kitten's navel. Great care must be taken that the cord is not pulled away from the kitten, or a severe umbilical hernia will result. Ideally, the cord should be severed by pinching it between the nails of one's thumb and forefinger, but an inexperienced novice may find it easier to cut the cord with sterilised scissors. A little blood may leak, but not enough to cause damage.

It is very important to check that after every kitten the placenta or after-birth is passed. Normally the queen will eat this, so it is necessary to watch events carefully. If a placenta is retained the breeder cannot do anything at the time apart from gently massaging the queen's abdomen. But the veterinary surgeon should be informed and he will probably give an injection of Pituitrin to cause the uterus to eject the placenta. If it remains in the uterus for longer than a few hours severe infection can be set up and the queen will refuse all food, develop a fever and become obviously ill.

If the litter is a large one, it is a wise plan to remove some of the newly-born kittens to a well-blanketed warm box with a well-covered hot water bottle in it, so that she can concentrate on the other kittens still to be born. However, the separated kittens should be kept out of earshot of the queen, or she will become agitated and try to jump out of her box.

Once the last kitten is born the queen seems to know that her ordeal is over, for she usually cleans herself all over, gathers the

78

kittens to her and settles down for a good sleep. Before she does so, she should be offered a drink of warm Carnation milk with added glucose. Once she has had a sleep she will be ready to have her usual meal, which should be fairly light for the first day after parturition.

The Abys, Turkish and Rex cats are normally ideal mothers, but very occasionally the latter's milk may be deficient in quantity or quality. A contented litter of kittens will sleep most of the time for the first fortnight, but if they are hungry they will be constantly crying and restless.

Then the breeder has to make a decision – and a quick one. Should the kittens have a foster-mother or should they be hand-reared? A foster-mother can usually be found through one's veterinary surgeon or through the R.S.P.C.A. When the kittens are introduced to the foster it must be done very carefully, as many fosters are suspicious of the peculiar-smelling babies. It is best to express a little of the milk gently from the foster-mother's teats and to rub this over the kittens. They should then be introduced to her through her back legs, so that they pick up her scent before she can lick them. In this way she will usually accept them readily.

If, however, a foster-mother cannot be found, then an attempt must be made to hand-feed the kittens. This is a tremendous task, as the kittens must be fed two-hourly throughout the day and night for the first three weeks. There are several methods by which the kittens can be fed. Special kitten-feeding bottles are now available, or the milk mixture can be given by a graduated dropper (the dropper from an Abidec Vitamin bottle is ideal).

We have tried both methods with varying degrees of success, as the great danger with either is that some of the liquid may enter the respiratory tract, causing inhalation pneumonia. A well-known veterinary surgeon has found that an artist's medium-sized paint-brush, dipped into milk mixture and placed on the kitten's tongue, is an ideal method. This has worked miraculously! The kittens like the feeling of the brush and start sucking at once. At first four paint-brushfuls every two hours are sufficient for the tiny kittens.

Several milk foods are available, but we have found the most successful to be Carnation milk, diluted three parts of milk to one part of boiling water with $\frac{1}{2}$-teaspoon of glucose added for each feed. Of course, all the utensils used, and the paint-brush, must be sterilised by boiling before being used.

In addition to the actual feeding, the kitten's abdomen must be massaged gently after each feed to promote digestion and passing of urine and faeces. However, if the mother is fit she will gladly attend to the tasks of cleaning and massaging her babies.

It is wonderfully satisfying to hand-rear a litter, but one does need a constitution of iron and an understanding human family who will tolerate canned foods quickly prepared for a few weeks.

Sexing a kitten is most easily done very shortly after birth, when the difference between the sexes is very obvious. Within a few hours of birth the genital area becomes slightly swollen and if the breeder is a novice the task is best left until the age of about three weeks when the differences again are more easily recognisable (see diagrams). In the female the anus and the vaginal and urethral apertures are situated close to one another, but in the male there is a space of about half an inch between the anal aperture and the urethra. Also, quite soon after birth tiny swellings are noticeable around the male urethra – these will later develop into the testicles.

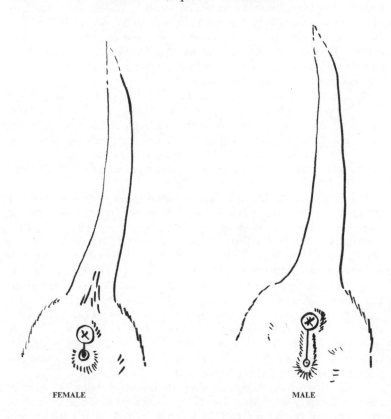

FEMALE   MALE

12   Rearing the Kittens

If all has gone well, the mother will do all that is necessary for the kittens for the first 3 to 4 weeks. It is the breeder's task to see that the bedding is kept clean (newspaper and a thick flannelette blanket make an ideal bed) and that the queen is well fed and groomed.

The kittens' eyes usually open at about 7—10 days. The first signs are tiny cracks appearing at the side of the eyelids, and in about three days the eyes are fully open. Occasionally the eyes may be a little sticky with a small amount of pus round the eyelids. If this occurs the eyes should be bathed carefully with Optrex solution and dried with clean cotton wool.

However, if the eyelids appear swollen and any discharge persists, the veterinary surgeon should be informed. There is a very common mild infection in cats that causes persistent sticky eyes and later conjunctivitis. This infection is due to a virus of the influenzal group, and can affect all cats in contact with it. In such a case the veterinary surgeon will probably prescribe an antibiotic to be given to both mother and kittens. Here again, the 'paint-brush method' is ideal for administering a small dose of a drug. The kitten may object and make terrible grimaces, but the drug goes down!

If the litter is large, it is a wise plan to start weaning the kittens at $3\frac{1}{2}$ weeks. Otherwise, $4\frac{1}{2}$ weeks is a good age to start weaning. At this stage the kittens may begin to soil their box, and the mother may become restless and try to move her family to what she considers a more suitable place. The family should then be moved to a large cardboard box, with an entrance door cut in one side, and a sanitary-tray filled with peat or shavings put near to the box. The bedding should now be changed daily.

The first weaning-meals should be evaporated milk, diluted three parts of milk to one of boiling water and a little added glucose. Each kitten should be stood on the floor and the warm milk offered in a dessertspoon. If a little milk is wiped on the kitten's nose it will usually start licking from the spoon, with many gasps and bubbles between licks! After several spoon-feeds the kitten should be gradually introduced to a saucer. Much patience is needed for this manoeuvre, as the kitten at first finds it unnatural to bend forward to the saucer.

81

Sherada Dilys—Red Abyssinian. Dam: Ch. Flume Atalanta. Sire: Ch. Shybu Koralai. Owned and bred by Mr. and Mrs. Warde

Photographer Mike Randall

Once a kitten can lap from a saucer, Farex should be added to the feed, using one teaspoon of Farex to each kitten.

By the time the kitten is $5\frac{1}{2}$ weeks old, it is ready to be introduced to more solid food. A little cooked plaice will usually be acceptable and it is easily digestible. This can soon be varied with scraped-lean beef, cooked rabbit and a little hard-boiled egg. Some of the well-known makes of strained baby food can also be given occasionally. The diet of a 6—10 weeks old kitten has been given in Chapter VII.

Kittens will drink plenty of fresh water and this should always be available. If considered necessary, additional vitamins should be given in the form of Kit-zyme Veterinary yeast tablets and Vitavel, half-teaspoon daily.

The suet so necessary to a Rex cat's coat should be introduced to the Rex diet at the age of nine weeks. The kittens do not take to it very readily, but if it is mixed well with the food their natural greediness soon overcomes their distrust of something new.

These kittens are usually house-trained by the time they are five weeks old. It is fascinating to watch the mother fussily pushing her offspring into the sanitary-tray and then scolding them until they have performed. At this stage it is particularly important to keep the trays spotlessly clean, as at rearing-time a kitten is especially susceptible to bacterial infection, and many cases of kitten diarrhoea are due to a build-up of E. Coli bacteria due to soiled sanitary-trays and unwashed floors.

If a litter does develop loose motions the veterinary surgeon should at once be informed. There are now wonderful drugs available which quickly kill the bacteria, but if diarrhoea is allowed to persist kittens very soon go downhill and may even die.

Once the kittens are house-trained it is time to ask the veterinary surgeon's advice on worming. If necessary, this should be carried out before vaccination (details on worming are to be found in Chapter 10).

After worming is the time for inoculation against Feline Infectious Enteritis and then comes the time for the kittens to go to their new homes. This is always a sad moment for the breeder. But if new owners have been carefully chosen it is wonderfully rewarding to hear their glowing reports about how the kittens have settled into their new homes. The most frequent comment is, 'I have had cats before, but until I had your kitten I never realised how affection can be bestowed by a pet.'

13   The Stud Cat

Male cats are exceptionally affectionate. For this reason alone it is unwise to consider having a male for stud-work unless the breeder can be certain that he can be kept well supplied with queens.

So often we have had enthusiastic novices ask for 'a pair of cats so that I can breed'. This idea is both impractical and cruel, for an entire male cannot live a normal life in a household. As soon as he becomes mature (around the age of eight months to a year) he will not only start wandering the countryside, but he will also 'spray' on the walls and in corners. The smell of tom-cat permeates the whole home and soon causes friends to make excuses when they are invited to visit. During his wanderings he will be attacked by every veteran tom in the district, for he will be a dangerous rival, and he will return home badly battle-scarred, if not severely injured. If there are no available queens an entire male may also become quite vicious, and it has been known for his owner to be quite badly injured in an attack by a frustrated male.

However, males make ideal pets if neutered at about the age of five months, though a male *can* be neutered at any time in his life with no ill-effects. It is now a law that neutering can only be performed under an anaesthetic, so the cat does not suffer at all from this minor operation.

The keen breeder may, however, decide to attempt stud-work. Having considered the best 'line' to choose for a stud, bearing in mind that breeders need an outcross where possible, plans must then be made for the housing of the stud.

It is essential that he has his own house and run in a spot fairly near the house, so that he can at least watch his owners, even if he cannot live with the family. The stud-house should be made of wood (cedar is best) and should measure at *least* 10 feet by 9 feet. This house will be the stud's home for life and it will also be the temporary home of his queens, so ample space is essential.

Since no stud-cat can live healthily in draughts, the house must be well-insulated with Fibreglass, over which is fixed hardboard or Laconite. If hardboard is used, it must be painted with an under-

Ideal Stud House and Run. Annelida 1971.

coat and then with two coats of a good, high-gloss paint, such as Walpamur's, Duradio or Trojax.

The floor should be of sectional wood and covered with a rot-proof easily-cleanable lino. One of the Vinyl linos are ideal. All joins in walls and floor should be sealed with decorator's tape before painting.

There should be at least two windows in the stud-house, with wide ledges beneath, so that the cat can sit and view his surroundings. There should also be at least two other ledges in the house, as a mated queen can be vicious, and the stud must be able to jump out of her way.

A 'cat-flap' is the ideal outlet to the run, as this is almost draught-proof and allows easy access to the run.

The queen will need a separate pen, which should be at least four   85 feet square and lined with a painted hardboard. It should have wire netting on two sides, so that the stud can talk to the queen after her arrival.

Heating of the stud-house can be by electrical tubular heaters and infra-red dull emitters. A stud is happiest if he can have an infra-red lamp over his bed, where he will necessarily spend many solitary hours. The heaters should be thermostatically controlled and the minimum temperature should be 58° F.

The run should be as large as possible, certainly not less than 18 feet by 12 feet. Ordinary one-inch wire mesh can be used on a wood framework, so long as the wood frame is well treated with Cuprinol. There should be two doors to the run, an external one and an inner-safety door, to ensure that a visiting queen does not escape.

If possible, the floor of the run should be of concrete, as this is easiest to keep clean, but a small square can be kept for grass.

All this will cost at least £70, but it is money well spent if it ensures the health and happiness of the stud and his queens.

A stud should be introduced gradually to his new quarters, being shut up there for an hour or two from a comparatively early age. Thus, when he finally has to remain permanently in his stud-house he will not fret so much. Throughout his working life he should be visited as often as possible and should be petted by all the family. My own Rex studs are used to the car and it is their greatest treat to go out on their harness and lead for a drive and perhaps a visit to the local pub. However, two studs can never be taken out together. Indeed, it is unwise to even let them meet at any time, as the most docile stud becomes a fighting maniac at the first scent of a rival male.

If possible the stud's first queen should be an experienced brood queen. He will doubtless be very keen, but a 'maiden' queen is always difficult and a queen who attacks a young stud can 'put him off' for life.

Even with an experienced queen he may not be successful at his first attempts at mating. It is wisest not to interfere, but the stud-owner must always be present at all matings. If after several attempts he has not succeeded in mating his queen she should be shut away again in her pen, while he has a rest and a feed.

Once he has successfully mated a queen, he will probably be keen for more, but no more than three matings should be allowed for a young stud. Always the queen should be either shut away in her pen between matings, or allowed a run by herself in the run.

86   A stud is usually ready for his first queen at about 11 months of

Turkish Cat "Van Hukre". Owner—Mrs. Russell.   *Photographer Anne Cumbers*

age, though some may not be fully mature until about 15 months or even later. During the first six months of stud-work, the stud should not be allowed more than one queen a month. An over-worked stud can become sterile at the age of two years, and this is a tragedy for both stud and owner. If all goes well for six months then the stud can have one queen a fortnight for a further six months. After this it is quite normal for a stud to cope happily with two queens a week. Unfortunately, there are still too few of these queens available and the stud's problem is often frustration due to lack of a satisfying love-life.

At all times the stud must have a very adequate diet with plenty of fresh raw meat with some raw eggs. An undernourished stud soon loses weight and also loses interest in his queens.

After the visit of each queen it is important to thoroughly disinfect the queen's pen. No matter how careful one is, there is always the risk of infection, and so a regular check-up by the veterinary surgeon is advisable.

The stud-owner should keep a careful register of all queens received, and when litters arrive the kittens should be recorded against the queen's name. Most queen-owners are interested in the breed and readily inform the stud-owner of the arrival of the kittens.

Stud-work brings many friends. Novice stud-owners should not be disheartened if it also occasionally brings enemies, as there is always a certain amount of jealousy of very successful studs. The affection of a healthy stud and the interest in the arrival of new litters of kittens is ample compensation for minor jealousies, and the knowledge that the history of a new breed is being made is perhaps the most satisfying part of the breeding of these cats.

14 Neutering and Spaying

As we mentioned in an earlier chapter, it is wise to have a kitten neutered at an early age, unless it is intended as a breeding animal. In fact, it is safe to neuter a healthy cat at any age between four months and twenty years!

It is not advocated before the age of four months, as the sexual organs would not be sufficiently mature and also all animals must be neutered under an anaesthetic, and there is an element of danger in using an anaesthetic on a very young kitten.

The term 'castration' is the correct one for neutering a male, and to neuter a female is to 'spay' her. Veterinary surgeons have reported that they have been asked to 'fillet' a young queen! This is an apt if not correct description!

The castration of a male is a very simple operation. He is given a light anaesthetic, and usually the hairs are plucked from the scrotum. The testicles are swabbed with disinfectant and held so that the skin is tense. The substance is cut with a blade and the testicle literally 'shelled' out by a gentle tug. It is discarded and the same operation is carried out on the second testicle. In this way only two incisions are necessary, and in a young cat no stitches are needed. In an older cat a veterinary surgeon will probably have to use a few stitches to prevent any possible bleeding.

Following this operation the cat is awake and ready to play after an hour, and usually demanding an extra large feed, as he will have had to starve for 12 hours before the operation.

In a few cases, a male cat may be a monorchid (only one testicle descended) or a cryptorchid (neither testicle descended). Either condition precludes the cat from any shows for entire males. Castration is also more difficult, as it will involve an abdominal surgical opening, but this is no problem in the hands of a skilled veterinary surgeon.

The spaying of a female kitten or cat is a slightly more major operation, but it is not likely to endanger the life of the cat. Nowadays the uterus and ovaries can be safely removed through an incision no longer than two inches. The fur is normally shaved off after the anaesthetic is given, and the incision is made either in the flank of the cat, or under her abdomen if she is not feeding kittens. The organs are rapidly located and ligatures applied before they are removed. In this case the ligatures would be of the slowly absorbing type, while the skin ligatures are usually of nylon.

Following the operation, the little female may be rather sleepy but will be asking for her food by the end of the day. She should be discouraged from jumping around for as long as possible. The stitches are usually removed after 10 days. Occasionally a queen will bite at the stitches, so she should be kept under observation for the first few days.

It is a great pity that all breeders do not advise their kittens' new owners to have the kitten neutered at an early age. An entire male is constantly involved in fights, arriving home with a torn ear or a leg abscess as a result of a bite. He is also a constant worry to the few owners of queens which are kept for breeding.

An entire female may also be involved in fights, but she is more likely to produce a large litter of kittens at an age as early as seven months. At that age, the queen's call may pass unnoticed by her owner, but local toms seem to get the message by some grapevine known only to them, and will travel miles to be on the spot for the unsuspecting maiden queen!

One still occasionally hears people say that 'neutering is cruel – not natural' and it is often difficult to persuade such people that it is only *they* who are being cruel by endangering the life of their pet.

15 Grooming and Care of the Cat

Part A: Grooming Rex Cats

Of all the many breeds of cats the Rex are the easiest to groom. Since they do not have guard-hairs they do not shed their coats regularly like the Short-Haired and Long-Haired breeds. For this reason they are particularly favoured by cat-lovers who live in apartments.

Normally, regular 'hand-grooming' is all that is required to keep a Rex coat looking soft and shining. This means that the hand is run over the coat, literally from head to tail. All that may come away after this treatment is a little light down. Nevertheless, a Rex cat or kitten should be combed with a close-toothed metal comb once a week, to ensure that it has not picked up any fleas. It is unlikely that a cat living in an apartment will pick up fleas, but those living in the country with access to a garden (where there may be hedgehogs) or to other cats, are almost certain to collect a flea or two at some time. The presence of fleas can easily be detected by the fine, hard 'flea-dirt' found at the root of the hairs.

The weekly comb should be accompanied by a weekly ear-cleaning session. No cat enjoys this process but if it is carried out gently from early kitten-days the cat usually accepts it with resignation! The 'cotton-buds' obtained from most chemists are ideal for cleaning ears. They can be used dry or moistened with a little olive oil. The presence of ear-mites should be suspected if the ear contains a dark-coloured wax instead of the normal honey-coloured exudate.

Grooming a Rex for shows entails a little more trouble, as a superbly-groomed Rex is likely to earn an extra point from a careful judge. A coloured Rex benfits from one or two 'bran baths' before a show. To give this, a small amount of bran (of the type used to feed rabbits) should be well-warmed in the oven.

When it feels pleasantly warm to the hand, the cat should be placed on a table in the kitchen (or any room in which there is no carpet) and the bran rubbed lightly into the coat along the back and tail, and over the abdominal area. It should be left on for as long as possible, but this will be quite a short time, as the cat will be shaking itself vigorously after the treatment! The coat should then be brushed with a soft, natural-bristle brush, and given a final polish with a silk handkerchief or old nylon stocking.

White Rex present a somewhat different problem, and the only really satisfactory way to present a white Rex in sparkling condition is to bath it on the evening before the show. However, the cat should have had an occasional bath several times before a show-date or it may be badly frightened.

It is easiest to bath a Rex cat in a sink, using water that is a little above human blood-heat (remembering that a cat's normal temperature is higher than that of a human). One of the reliable makes of human baby-shampoos is excellent, as, if any should run into the cat's eyes it will not cause any irritation. The shampoo should be applied after the coat has been made thoroughly wet and should be rubbed in gently. The cat should then be held on the floor while the rinsing-water is run into the sink. When it is at the correct temperature the cat should be thoroughly rinsed and then wrapped in a warm bath-towel (see picture of Champion Annelida Icicle). After a good towelling the cat should be allowed to curl up near a warm fire or radiator – he should never be allowed to be in a draught, as he can easily be chilled at this time. A drink of warm milk is a pleasant reward after a bath, and the cat soon accepts the whole affair as part of a show life.

When the coat is completely dry it can be lightly powdered and then carefully brushed. If a cat is found to have powder in its coat while at the show it will be disqualified.

A final mention must be made of the possibility of 'stud-tail' in the Rex cat. Unfortunately, this unsightly bare patch at the base of the tail is NOT confined to stud-cats and can be found in any adolescent or adult Rex cat. It may happen in other varieties, too, appearing as scurf or a greasy patch, at the base of the tail.

If a cat shows any evidence of this trouble the tail must be cleaned daily with surgical spirit until all the extra secretion of grease is removed. If it is then kept dry and clean the condition should not recur.

The novice should not be disheartened at the thought of so much show-preparation. The sight of an elegant, shining Rex cat is sufficient reward for the extra trouble, and if a few red cards appear on the cat's pen the owner will be proud and excited.

Top. Annelida Columbine (Cornish Rex Kitten) being groomed with soft bristle brush. Columbine now owned by Mrs. Falconer, Pretoria, South Africa   *Photographer Anne Cumbers*

Bottom. Show preparation—Champion Annelida Icicle (Devon Rex) is watched by White Cornish Rex. Owned and bred by Mrs. Ashford

Photographer Anne Cumbers

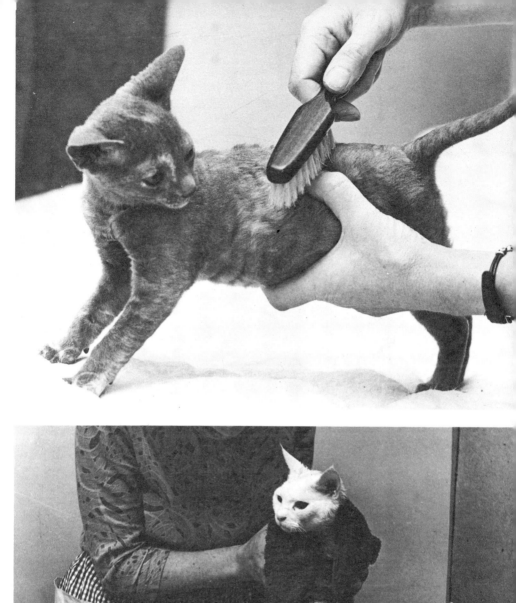

16 Exhibiting and Cat Shows

Three types of shows are held in this country under the auspices of the Governing Council of the *Cat Fancy*.

There are Championship shows at which challenge certificates issued by the Council are given to the winners of the adult open breed classes, provided they reach a certain standard. A challenge certificate may be withheld should a judge consider a cat to be unworthy of this honour, but it is necessary for another judge to agree and to sign the judging slip as well. A cat winning three such certificates at three Championship shows under three different judges becomes entitled to be called a Champion. A neutered or spayed cat may become a Premier by winning premier certificates at three shows under three different judges.

The next type of show is known as a Sanction Show. It is run on similar lines to those of the Championship show, and, indeed, is looked on as a rehearsal by the club running it, hoping eventually to be granted a licence for a Championship one. Challenge certificates are not given at Sanction shows, but otherwise there is very little difference between the two.

The third type is the Exemption show. The number of cats entered is usually small and such a show is ideal for beginners to start exhibiting. The rules are not so strict, no challenge certificates are given and the whole atmosphere is far more relaxed and the competition less fierce than at the larger shows. The judges, too, are not so rushed and may be willing to talk to novices about the potentialities of their cats. The penning and vetting procedure is as for other shows and will enable a beginner to see how his cat reacts when being handled by the judges and stewards. A cat that resents handling and is bad-tempered should not be exhibited again.

It is not always easy to know when and where cat shows are being held. A list is published each year by the Governing Council and may be obtained for a few pence from the Secretary. Shows are advertised in *Fur and Feather*, the official organ of the Council, a weekly periodical which may be ordered through a newsagent, and *Cats* magazine, a bi-monthly periodical published by H. Clover, 68 The Dale, Widley, Portsmouth, PO7 5DE. This is available on subscription only. Shows are usually advertised in some of the national newspapers and some of the locals, but this will be too late to be of use to the would-be exhibitor. There is so much work to be done in connection with the running of even the smallest show that schedules are issued well in advance, with the date for sending in entries closing many weeks before the day of the show. The most important task for the show manager is the preparation of the show catalogue for the printer, as all entries must be in this in full, and the printer needs the copy well in advance.

Entry forms and show rules are sent out with the schedule and all should be read through most carefully. The schedule contains particulars of the various classes. It is not necessary to belong to any club to enter a show, but many clubs put on classes at other clubs' shows for their members alone, and there is a reduced entry charge if one is a member of the club organising the show. The choice of classes is numerous, but the most important one is the Open or Breed class, for which, if for adults, a challenge certificate may be given. It is usual to enter at least two, but not more than 12, classes. There are classes for Kittens, Novices, Senior and Junior cats, among many others, with a special class for Novice Exhibitors. A definition of the classes will be found at the beginning of the schedule.

Before even considering entering for any show, a check should be made that the cat or kitten is registered and has been transferred to the person exhibiting it. The details as set out on the registration form are necessary for filling in the entry form. It is also advisable to make sure that the animal has been inoculated against Feline Infectious Enteritis. If not already inoculated, this should be done at least three weeks before the show.

Some shows, such as the National Cat Club Show, have special classes for household pets, and these must not be pedigree or registered, and, of course, cannot compete against pedigree cats. The pedigree cats are judged on their closeness to the required standard and general condition, while the pets are judged on temperament and condition. There are special classes for Champions and Premiers only, and the winners of these classes, subject to specified conditions, may eventually become Grand Champions and Grand Premiers. Pedigree neuters and spays may not compete against entire cats in any classes.

Kittens must be at least three months old before they may be exhibited, but if there are classes for litters, dependent on the time of year, they may be two to three months old. A kitten becomes an adult on the day it is nine months old and can then enter in the open class.

Shows are well filled and entries frequently have to be returned, so it is advisable to send in the completed form, together with the correct money, well before the closing date.

Entries are not usually acknowledged. If an acknowledgement is required, a stamped addressed postcard should also be enclosed.

Approximately two weeks before the show day the show manager sends out to all accepted entries a small white numbered tally and a vetting-in card. No exhibit is permitted to enter into the show hall until it has been thoroughly examined by one of the officiating veterinary surgeons to make sure that it is in good condition. Fleas in the fur, dirty ears, ulcers in the mouth, a high temperature or any other signs of illness will mean refusal of the entry. There are usually a few pens in a separate room, which is used as the hospital, but rather than leave an animal penned there all day with other sick animals, it is advisable, if possible, to take home any exhibit that has been refused admission.

The cat must be taken to the hall in an escape-proof container, not carried in the arms or on a lead. Other requirements are a clean warm white blanket, free of markings or distinguishing features, a white litter tray, drinking and feeding dishes. The white tally must be worn around the exhibit's neck on a piece of plain white tape. In very cold weather hot water bottles are allowed, but they must be well concealed under the blanket. Food and drink should be taken, but no dishes may be left in the pen during judging.

The number on the tally corresponds to the number on the pen provided for the cat, and once it has been passed by the veterinary surgeon it may be taken into the hall and placed in the pen. Before taking the cat out of the basket, the pen should be wiped all over with mild non-toxic disinfectant. The white blanket should be placed in the pen and the litter tray filled with peat moss, which is provided in the hall, or torn-up newspaper, if preferred by the cat. The numbered tally should be securely fastened around the neck, but not so tightly as to hurt, and the cat given a quick last-minute grooming and left to await the judge. The container may be placed under the pen, with any name on it well hidden.

Judging usually starts about ten o'clock and goes on for most of the day. At the National Cat Club show at the Olympia the public are admitted into the hall all day, but at other shows they cannot come in until about 12.30 p.m. Some halls have galleries, and exhibitors are allowed to watch from there.

Accompanied by a steward carrying a small table and some form of disinfectant and a towel, the judge goes to each pen, and examines each exhibit individually. The results are noted in her judging book

96

Mallorca Sicat. The first Siamese-patterned Devon Rex to be born in
England. Owner—Mrs. A. Ashford. Breeder—Mrs. K. Lidyard
Photographer Anne Cumbers

and eventually the slips showing the prize-winners are displayed on an award board at the side of the hall. Once the public are admitted catalogues are for sale, and it is as well for an exhibitor to check through to make sure that her cat is entered in the catalogue in its correct classes. Any errors should be pointed out to the Show Manager.

In the early afternoon prize cards are put on the pens and it is then permissible to feed the cat, if so desired, although some exhibitors prefer not to, giving only water to drink until they get home.

Most shows close at 5.30 p.m. and the owners must be there well before that time, ready to take the cat home, as the pens are taken down immediately after the show.

The prize money is not paid out at the show. Indeed, it is several weeks before it is sent out, as all entries are checked from the catalogue by the Registrars of the Governing Council of the Cat Fancy. Should any of the information given on the entry form be found to be incorrect disqualification may follow, which means loss of prize-money and entry fees. So before sending in all entries should be double-checked.

Particular care should be taken of the cat on its return home. Even if inoculated against Feline Infectious Enteritis it should be isolated from other cats and kittens for a few days, as it is possible it may have picked up some infection. Wiping all over the fur, around the mouth and eyes with a mild solution of a non-toxic disinfectant is advocated by some breeders, also the giving of a little whisky or brandy in milk. If the cat has not eaten all day it should be given a meal of some favourite dish and left to sleep in a warm draught-proof room.

If you are interested in exhibiting and hoping to become a steward and eventually a judge, most show managers are only too willing to accept offers of help at the shows, which is the only way to begin. Putting up prize slips, marking prize cards and helping in any way required teaches show procedure and is the first step towards being asked to be a steward. Many years of acting as a steward, together with breeding and exhibiting high quality cats and kittens, are the very necessary qualifications required before anyone is considered experienced enough to be selected as a judge.

17 The Governing Council of the Cat Fancy

Over the centuries unusual-looking cats had been displayed as side shows at county fairs and agricultural shows, but in 1871 Mr. Harrison Weir 'conceived the idea that it would be well to hold "Cat Shows" so that the different breeds, colours, markings, etc., might be more carefully attended to, and the domestic cat, sitting in front of the fire, would then possess a beauty and an attractiveness to its owner unobserved and unknown because uncultivated heretofore'. He held his first show at the Crystal Palace and the public flocked in to see how beautiful cats could be and how they differed greatly in colouring and coat patterns. Further shows were organised not only in London but in other parts of the country and proved most successful. This was the beginning of the ever-growing interest in pedigree cats throughout the world today, known collectively as the Cat Fancy.

It was soon appreciated that by choosing different coloured males and females and breeding from their progeny it was possible to produce kittens of a desired colour to order. Eventually it was realised that to do this it would be necessary to keep some kind of a record of the parentage if the breeding was to be kept pure. The National Cat Club was formed in 1887 by a number of fanciers interested in showing and breeding cats. In 1893 the Club issued a Stud Book 'the only reliable source of information concerning the pedigree of cats'. Eventually the Club also kept a National Register of Cats and became the first registering body, being responsible for the classification of the various breeds, also approving shows held under its jurisdiction, granting Championships, and 'doing all in its power to protect and advance the interests of Cats'.

A number of clubs began in other parts of the country, but the National remained the sole registering body until 1898, when Lady Marcus Beresford founded a rival organisation known as The Cat Club. The latter, however, proved to be short-lived, but there was still disagreement amoung the various clubs, and in 1910 The Governing Council of the Cat Fancy was formed, with the National Cat Club waiving all rights of registration, but remaining the premier cat club of Britain.

The Governing Council was, and still is, composed of delegates from the affiliated clubs from all over England, Scotland, Wales and Northern Ireland. To be affiliated, a club must have a membership of at least 50, and if requesting representation, of at least 100, then having the right to send a delegate to attend the meetings of the Council as the club's representative to look after its interests. The delegate is elected annually by the members of the club, and it is from the delegates that the Chairman of the Council and the Officers, who sit for one year, are elected. It meets at least four times a year, but more frequently recently, so great has been the increase in cat affairs. A number of sub-committees are also elected annually, such as the Executive, the Finance and the Cat-Care committee, among others, all having specified duties to carry out. The delegates give their services free.

The Council's aims are to improve and advise on cat breeding and cat welfare. It classifies cat breeds, approving and recognising standards, granting breed numbers for new varieties as the need arises. Before recognition is considered the particular cats must have at least three generations of pure breeding behind them. It is no easy thing to create a new variety entailing years of selective breeding, with many kittens that fail to comply with the set breeding programme having to be neutered and sold as pets.

Approval is given for dates of the various Champion, Exemption and Sanction shows held under licence granted by the Council, with the issuing of Challenge and Premier certificates to the appropriate shows (see Chapter on Exhibiting and Cat Shows).

The Council registers prefixes, which are approved distinguishing names granted to fanciers wishing to go in for breeding and wanting to have their own cattery name. On payment of the required fee the breeder has the sole use of such a prefix for life, and may use this before the personal name given to any kitten bred by him. It is most useful in that kittens constantly winning at the shows and bearing a certain prefix will be eagerly sought after.

As well as registering kittens and cats on payment of the required fee, the Council also issues transfer certificates, certifying change of ownership. A small charge is also made for these. If required, certified export pedigrees may be obtained from the Council when cats are exported from this country. The prices for these will be given on application to the Secretary.

The council employ a paid Secretary for general duties and two Registrars who are responsible for the registrations and transfers.

A booklet is issued by the Council setting out in full the approved standard of points for the recognised varieties. The Standard of Points allocates 100 points for certain characteristics considered desirable in an ideal specimen of a recognised variety. Such a cat has

Ch. Flume Atalanta—Red Abyssinian. Owner—Mr. and Mrs. Warde
Photographer Mike Randall

never existed, but the points are apportioned between the head and body shape, the colour and shape of the eyes, the fur colour, the markings or absence of them, and so on. It is impossible to breed a perfect cat that will conform in every way to the set standard, but many seen at the shows come very close to it, and it is always a challenge and the aim of every breeder to produce a cat that will be as perfect as possible. The Standard is also the yardstick on which to judge for all the approved Governing Council judges.

The Council also publishes annually a list of stud cats, giving the names and addresses of owners who are willing to accept female cats for mating to their males. In addition it publishes at regular intervals a Stud Book, listing the various cats that have obtained Championship status and setting out details of current prize-winning cats. An 101 annual list of cat shows held under the jurisdiction of the Council may be obtained from the Secretary. A list of the various affiliated cat clubs, together with the names and addresses of their secretaries, is also obtainable.

A number of the affiliated clubs are specialist societies dealing with matters relating to specific varieties, such as the Abyssinian Cat Club. This Club looks after the interests of Abyssinians alone and appoints judges, who have to be approved by the Governing Council, for this variety. Non-specialist clubs are interested in all breeds, but do not have the power to appoint judges.

Before buying a pedigree kitten the would-be purchaser should check that the kitten has been registered and ask to see the numbered registration form issued by the Governing Council. This is most important, as it is impossible to exhibit at a show unless the parentage and the registration number is known. Breeders should give a pedigree with the kitten with these details, and should also supply a signed transfer form which has to be sent to the Registrar, together with the fee. Before any kitten can be exhibited by a new owner it should have been transferred from the old, at least three weeks before the date of the show. If this is not done, it will be disqualified.

After a show, before the prize money is paid out, a copy of the catalogue is sent to the Secretary for checking to make sure that all the details given about the various entries are quite correct. If incorrect in any detail, such as wrong age, disqualification may follow.

Apart from disqualification for incorrect entries, the Governing Council of the Cat Fancy has the power to censor and suspend breeders for any serious violation of the Council's rules and regulations regarding shows, showing and cat welfare generally.

The Secretary to the Governing Council is Mrs. W. Davis, Dovefields, Petworth Road, Witley, Surrey. Details of the various publications and services, and prices will be sent by her on receipt of a stamped addressed envelope.

The Registrar for all varieties (excepting Siamese) is Miss P. Saunders, 50 Marine Parade, Brighton BN2 IPH, Sussex. Forms for registering Abyssinians, Rex and Turkish cats, among others, may be obtained from her on receipt of a stamped addressed envelope.

THE AFFILIATED CAT CLUBS

There are a number of cat clubs and Societies throughout the country whose members share a common interest in pedigree cats. The majority of these clubs cater for all varieties, but there are a number of Specialists Clubs for particular breeds, several looking after the interests of the cats mentioned in this book:—

102

ABYSSINIAN CAT CLUB
Secretary:
Mrs. I. Earnshaw, Heatherpine, Curridge, Nr. Newbury, Berkshire.
COLOURPOINT, REX-COATED AND A.O.V.
Secretary:
Mrs. B. Porter, 22 Doggetts Court, Brookhill Road, East Barnet, Herts.
(This Club looks after the interests of the Turkish cats as well as those mentioned in its name.)
REX CAT CLUB
Secretary:
Mrs. M. Shrouder, Pussy Willow, Ringwood Road, Three Legged Cross, Dorset.

For addresses of any other clubs write to the Secretary of the Council for complete list. It is not necessary to live in a particular district to be a member of a club, nor is it compulsory to belong to a club to exhibit at a show, but is an advantage in that members of clubs putting on the show may enter at reduced rates.

18 General Information

Holiday times and Boarding Catteries

Before considering buying a kitten it is as well to remember that arrangements will have to be made for its care and wellbeing when you go away on holiday, even if only for a few days, as a cat or kitten cannot be left without someone to look after it. A friendly neighbour may be willing to come in several times a day to feed it, change the toilet tray, and make sure all is well, and then the cat will be able to stay in its own home with little disturbance to it. It should not be allowed to wander in and out of the house as it pleases while the owner is away, unless you are sure that it will not roam. Many cats pine at such times and wander away looking for their owners.

There are a number of boarding catteries throughout the country these days catering entirely for cats, and having small houses with separate runs. It is not always easy to find one near to you, but the local R.S.P.C.A. inspector, officials of other animal welfare societies, or your veterinary surgeon may be able to help you by supplying names, or there may be advertisements in the local papers. One that has been thoroughly recommended is usually the best, but although catteries may now only function under licence it should always be inspected before a definite booking is made, as some still leave a lot to be desired. When inspecting insist on seeing the actual houses and runs where the animals are boarded. If the cattery is well run, you may be sure that bookings will have to be made well in advance; some owners, if they are pleased, booking their pet in at the end of one holiday for the next.

When taking your cat along you will probably be asked to bring with you a certificate showing that it has been inoculated against Feline Infectious Enteritis, and may also have to supply a vet's certificate saying that the animal is in perfect health. This is not only to safeguard your pet but is a protection for the fellow boarders. It is also advisable to take a diet sheet giving details of any particular likes and dislikes in the way of food.

If you intend leaving the cat at the boarding cattery on the way to your holiday make sure that it is shut up indoors in a safe place many hours before you are ready to depart. Cats have an uncanny way of

104

knowing what is going on, and the mere sight of a suitcase is sufficient for some to disappear for the day, upsetting all the arrangements.

You may be asked to pay in advance or leave a deposit. The
exact date of your return should be specified, as if the cattery is
booked up for the season delaying your return for a day or two,
although it may not seem to matter to you, may inconvenience
another owner, if the run is still in use when he arrives with his cat.

A few hotels may accept cats, but not very many, and certainly
not unneutered male cats. A neuter that is trained to walk on a lead
and used to a toilet tray may be accepted, but inquiries must always
be made in advance about the situation.

Antalya Anatolia & Van Bayan. Owned and bred by Miss Lushington
Photographer Sonia Halliday

Quarantine

Cats cannot be taken with their owners on holidays abroad. At least, they can go, but it means a stay of six months in an approved quarantine kennel on your return and an injection against rabies when it arrives and when it leaves quarantine. As cats dislike such confinement it is far better to make arrangements to leave them in this country if you are going away for only a short period. If you are going away for a few years or returning to this country after a period abroad and wish to bring your cat back with you, quarantine is inevitable. There is no free entry of cats into this country. All have to go into quarantine at approved kennels kept under strict supervision, and cats are met at the port of arrival and collected by specified carrying agents. A licence is necessary before the cat is allowed in. This strict control is necessary to prevent a cat suffering from rabies bringing the disease into the country. The Ministry of Agriculture, Animal Health Division, Hook Rise, Tolworth, Surbiton, Surrey, England, will supply a list of approved quarantine kennels, also names of suitable carrying agents. The cost does vary, and it is advisable to write to the kennels well beforehand to find out the cost, which for the six months period could be as much as £100. It should be remembered, however, that you would have the cost of feeding the cat all that time if it was with you, so the cost is by no means prohibitive. Choose a quarantine kennel as near as possible to where you will be living. Cats may suffer mentally through long confinement, so every effort should be made to make at least one weekly visit during visiting hours, so that your cat does not forget you, and also so that you can make sure that all is well.

Many cats and kittens are exported from Britain to countries all over the world, each country having differing conditions regarding the entry of animals, and it is advisable to contact the Ministry of Agriculture, address as above, for information on this. Some countries have no quarantine for cats from Britain, while others have varying periods.

ANIMAL WELFARE SOCIETIES

There are a number of excellent welfare societies all over the country looking after the interests and wellbeing of various animals; in one case specialising in cats. Some are shelters taking in unwanted and stray animals; others have clinics specialising in the treatment of the sick. Most issue leaflets dealing with the care of cats, which cost only a few pence and a stamped and addressed envelope. It is not possible to give names and addresses of all these organisations, but a few are listed below:

THE CATS PROTECTION LEAGUE, 29 Church Street, Slough, Bucks, has various branches throughout the country, and is always seeking good homes for unwanted cats and kittens, being very particular as to where they are placed, and painlessly destroying any it is unable to place. The League will also arrange for the spaying and neutering of cats and kittens under a voucher scheme, the owner paying according to his means.

THE R.S.P.C.A., 105 Jermyn Street, London, S.W.1. This society has many clinics throughout the country, and the addresses of the inspectors may be found in local telephone directories. The Society runs its own boarding kennels and clinics where veterinary treatment and advice on cats is given free to anyone who cannot afford to pay.

THE BLUE CROSS SOCIETY, 1 Hugh Street, Victoria, London, S.W.1, runs hospitals, clinics and homes for the care and treatment of sick animals. The Society tries to find good homes for stray and unwanted cats, and treatment is given free to sick cats, whose owners cannot pay the fees.

THE PEOPLE'S DISPENSARY FOR SICK ANIMALS, P.D.S.A. House, South Street, Dorking, Surrey, has permanent and mobile dispensaries in Britain and some countries abroad. Supported entirely by voluntary contributions, free treatment is given to sick cats and other animals whose owners are unable to pay.

It is possible to purchase cardboard cat boxes from the branches of most of these societies and organisations. These are ideal for carrying cats if they are sick and for travelling with their owners, but they are not suitable for sending unaccompanied by train. It may also be possible to buy from them safe elastic collars suitable for cats.

CATS AND THE LAW

There are various laws in Britain relating to animals, and although more frequently than not cats are not mentioned individually, they have the same rights as other animals. Briefly, they are protected against unnecessary suffering, deliberate fright, torture, injuring, being abandoned or stolen, nor may they be shot for trespass alone.

The neutering of a kitten over the age of six months must be carried out under an anaesthetic, although many owners insist on it no matter what the age. An anaesthetic must be administered for any vital operation on a cat.

Any one putting down poison for the destruction of vermin must take all precautions to make sure that it will not harm cats. It should be noted that some poison advertised as safe does have an accumulative effect, preventing coagulation of the blood, particularly if the animals eat rats and mice that have consumed the poison.

TRAVEL

Some cats enjoy travelling in their owner's cars, others dislike it intensely, dribbling or panting all the time. If travel is unavoidable for such cats, they should be in a cardboard container (see Animal Welfare Societies), or in a cat basket or box, never loose in the car. If he considers it advisable, a veterinary surgeon may administer a tranquilliser, but some cats suffer a reaction from this. This is the reason for the notice in show schedules to the effect that 'Any cat found to be suffering from the effects of drugs on entry or at any time during the Show will be subject to expulsion from the Show on the authority of the Veterinary Surgeon'.

Even cats that love travelling should be kept on a lead or harness or in a box, as there is always the danger that they may, by playing or jumping about, distract the driver.

Cats travelling by train with their owner should be on a harness or lead or in a basket, but if unaccompanied they must be in an adequate-sized container, clearly marked 'Live Cat – with care'. If the weather is cold, there should be a hot water bottle under a thick blanket for warmth, and the container should be draught-proof, but provision must be made for adequate ventilation.

There are different regulations regarding travelling by air, and before taking or sending any cat this way it is advisable to check with the air company about their specific requirements.

Cats are carried on buses and coaches only if permitted to do so by the conductor or driver, and permission may not always be given. The cats should be in baskets or boxes and it should be realised that several cats in their containers, if being taken to a show, can be quite a hazard during rush hours. Some companies make a small charge for carrying cat baskets and boxes. On the tubes and Underground cats may be carried in adequate containers.

SPECIALISTS AND ALL-BREED CLUBS INTERESTED IN THE ABYSSINIAN, REX AND TURKISH VARIETIES

As from time to time there may be changes in the names and addresses of the secretaries of the clubs, these are not given, but an up-to-date list may be obtained from the Secretary of the Governing Council of the Cat Fancy, Dovefields, Petworth Road, Witley, Surrey – a stamped addressed envelope must be enclosed.

ABYSSINIAN CAT CLUB
BEDFORD AND DISTRICT CAT CLUB
CAPITAL LONGHAIR ASSOCIATION
CHESHIRE AREA CAT CLUB

COLOURPOINT, REX-COATED AND A.O.V. CLUB
CORNISH CAT ASSOCIATION
COVENTRY AND LEICESTER CAT CLUB
CROYDON CAT CLUB
EDINBURGH AND EAST OF SCOTLAND CAT CLUB
ESSEX CAT CLUB
GWYNEDD CAT CLUB
HERTS AND MIDDLESEX CAT CLUB
KENSINGTON KITTEN AND NEUTER CAT CLUB
KENTISH CAT SOCIETY
LANCS. AND N.W. COUNTIES CAT CLUB
LONG-HAIRED CAT CLUB
MERSEYSIDE CAT CLUB
MIDLAND COUNTIES CAT CLUB
NATIONAL CAT CLUB
NORTH EAST OF SCOTLAND CAT CLUB
NORTHERN COUNTIES CAT CLUB
NORTHERN IRELAND CAT CLUB
NOTTS AND DERBY CAT CLUB
PRESTON CAT CLUB
REX CAT CLUB
SCOTTISH CAT CLUB
SHORT-HAIRED CAT SOCIETY OF GREAT BRITAIN AND MANX
    CLUB INC.
SOUTHERN COUNTIES CAT CLUB
SOUTH WESTERN COUNTIES CAT CLUB
SUFFOLK AND NORFOLK CAT CLUB
SURREY AND SUSSEX CAT ASSOCIATION
THREE COUNTIES CAT SOCIETY
ULSTER CAT CLUB
WESSEX CAT CLUB
WEST OF ENGLAND AND SOUTH WALES CAT SOCIETY
YORKSHIRE COUNTY CLUB

19   Common Ailments

Pedigree cats are normally very healthy and hardy animals. But they are still prone to all the infectious diseases and are also not immune to the many parasites that prey on animals. There are several excellent books dealing with the treatment of sick cats, so I will not attempt to do more than outline the ailments that are most commonly found in any cat.

Before discussing feline illness, it is worth mentioning the person who will be caring for the sick cat, the veterinary surgeon. Many people do not realise that in the same way that some doctors specialise in child care and others in maternity work, so some veterinary surgeons specialise in the care of small animals, while others are expert in treating the large farm animals. Many people will call the nearest veterinarian and then complain bitterly that 'he was useless with my cat'.

While it is quite certain that no veterinary surgeon would be 'useless' with a cat, it is equally clear that some may not specialise in their treatment. The obvious answer is to ask the veterinary surgeon whether he is a small animal specialist or, if this seems difficult, the Secretary of the B.V.A., 7, Mansfield Street, London, W.1, will always supply the names of small animal specialists working in your area.

All veterinary surgeons are very busy people and a cat owner should be sure that the cat is really ill before asking for veterinary help. The symptoms should be clearly described, and, if possible, the temperature given. If the veterinary surgeon pays a home visit, the cat should be shut in a room to await his arrival. It must be very annoying for a busy veterinarian to have to chase a frightened animal round the house with the helpless owner standing by! It must be equally annoying when a cat owner gives her own diagnosis, having called for expert attention. Only a qualified person can be certain of the nature of the disease. If the cat owner can remember these few points, both veterinary adviser and client can have confidence in each other, and so the cat will have the best possible attention.

Feline Infectious Enteritis. In spite of the fact that kittens can now be inoculated against this terrible disease, it is still one of the chief killers of young cats. Infectious enteritis is a somewhat misleading name and the correct term 'feline panleucopaenia' is more descriptive as it means a disease in which the white blood cells (leucocytes) are greatly reduced in number. With a lowered number of leucocytes the cat is unable to fight the virus which causes the disease and death frequently results.

Although kittens are most susceptible to the disease, a cat of any age may contract it. It is a highly infectious disease which takes from 7 to 10 days to show itself after contact with infection. Unfortunately the symptoms are very varied and the onset is sudden, so a cat or kitten which suddenly refuses all food, looks 'hunched up', has an open 'staring' coat and a high temperature (the normal temperature of a cat varies between 101° F. and 102° F.) should immediately be suspect and should be examined by a veterinary surgeon without delay. There may be vomiting of a frothy colourless fluid and if the abdomen is touched the cat obviously appears to be in pain. There is rarely diarrhoea in the early stages.

The tragedy is that there is at the present no drug which will kill the attacking virus. The veterinary surgeon will give an antibiotic to combat any secondary infection that may cause pneumonia, and he will also be able to give large doses of subcutaneous glucose-saline to counteract the dehydration that is so characteristic of F.I.E. Nursing is of the greatest importance in this illness, as the cat is always very depressed, hating to feel dirty and unkempt, and wanting only to crawl into some cold draught to hasten the end. The care of a loved human being is invaluable, but it will mean a 24-hour nursing routine.

The cat must be kept warm and clean, and it must be given fluids. Although the veterinary surgeon will give subcutaneous fluid it is still necessary to give as much as possible by mouth. Even though the cat is desperately ill it will probably fight against fluids given by spoon. It must then be given either in a large eye-dropper or else by a hypodermic syringe. Whichever method is used, the dropper or syringe must be inserted into the mouth and *above* the tongue before the fluid is trickled down the throat. It is very important that the fluid is not squirted under the tongue, as the cat could then inhale the fluid, and, if it did not choke, inhalation pneumonia could result.

The veterinary surgeon will advise what is best to give, but usually glucose-saline or beaten egg-white and glucose are excellent. If the cat is unable to keep anything down, two drops of brandy given in a teaspoon of warm water half-an-hour before each feed will sometimes soothe the stomach.

Turkish Cat Swimming. Owned and bred by Miss Lushington

If the cat survives the first 48 hours, there is some hope that it may pull through. If it shows slight improvement and the fever drops it is wise to give fluid containing a high percentage of protein, such as Brand's Essence or the very excellent Protogest, which even sick cats seem to enjoy.

Convalescence after F.I.E. is always very slow, and much patience and affection is needed to persuade the cat that life is really worth living after all. Once again the veterinary surgeon will probably be able to give something to stimulate the appetite and produce a tonic effect. Once the cat tastes voluntarily some solid food (only highly-flavoured meat or fish is tempting) the battle is half-way to being won. During convalescence, if the cat can sit outside in a warm, sunny spot, it will not only be cheered, but the sun will be an added tonic.

One most important point with F.I.E. is that, even though the cat has recovered, the infection may still linger on his coat, and on the premises, for up to three months. If a cat has died, it would be very dangerous to bring any other cat into the house until three months has elapsed. During this time the owner should not attend a cat show or visit another cattery, as the virus can be carried on clothing. When possible, all clothing and bedding should be burnt, and the house completely scrubbed out with a disinfectant. Research workers at Bristol University advocate the use of pure Formalin (one teaspoon in a pint of water) as the most effective disinfectant after outbreaks of F.I.E. If it is possible to repaint all paintwork the possibility of infection remaining is greatly lessened.

It is a good plan to give all cats a 'booster' dose of F.I.E. vaccine each year, as this gives a certain immunity. I have seen a cat die, in great pain and despair, from this awful disease, and I know that no expense is too great to save a loved pet from such a horrible end.

Enteritis is the name used for any inflammation of the intestines. This is fairly common in kittens, but more infrequent in adult cats. It can be caused by over-eating, by eating unsuitable foods, by worm infestation, by forms of food poisoning due to salmonellosis, or by viral or bacterial infection.

Symptoms of enteritis are diarrhoea, which may be mucoid and blood-stained; abdominal pain, and sometimes, though not always, some degree of fever.

In all case of enteritis the cat should be examined by a veterinary surgeon when the first symptoms appear. He will possibly prescribe an antibiotic or one of the sulpha drugs, and will give detailed instructions about diet. The important point to remember is that the   113 cat's intestines are already inflamed and need to be rested, although it will still need nutrition. Anything given by mouth should be fluid and non-irritant. Beaten-up egg-white and glucose is ideal, followed by Brand's Essence or rabbit broth.

It is very important that the sanitary tray is kept scrupulously clean, because if the cause of diarrhoea is bacterial the bacteria can multiply very rapidly and can cause serious illness. It is normal for all humans and animals to have a certain amount of bacteria in the intestines, but if these reach a high level illness can follow, and this may be fatal if the infection spreads to the bloodstream.

I was once told by an elderly cat-breeder that castor oil is a sure way to cure diarrhoea in kittens. Fortunately I consulted my veterinary surgeon before using it, and he soon put me right on this subject! Castor oil should *never* be used for cats or kittens, as it masks the symptoms, making it impossible for the veterinarian to diagnose the trouble. Also, it tends to destroy any vitamins that are being digested by the cat. 'Old Wives' tales' like this must be responsible for a number of unnecessary kitten deaths.

Van Seftah Iskenderun, a Turkish cat. Owned and bred by Miss L. Lushington
Photographer Sonia Halliday

Gastritis is inflammation of the stomach and stomach-lining. This again is fairly common in kittens and can be caused by indigestion, by hairball, by poisons, or by viral or bacterial infection.

The kitten refuses its food and vomits frequently, at first any food that may still be in the stomach, and then yellow or white frothy vomit. It is obviously in some discomfort and even in pain, and it may have some fever.

As always, the veterinary surgeon should be consulted and the kitten should be kept very warm, as constant vomiting causes severe shock. Two drops of brandy in a teaspoon of warm water will help to settle the stomach. All solid foods should be withheld and again only bland fluids given. Even when the kitten appears to be feeling hungry, it should still be given only fluids for 24 hours.

Feline Infectious Peritonitis. This illness was first recognised in England in 1970 but records show that it was found in the U.S.A. in 1966. It is sometimes a chronic and almost always a fatal disease. It is both infectious and contagious and the incubation period is a long one – possibly as long as two months. It is caused by a virus.

In its early stages it is difficult to diagnose, especially as so few British veterinary surgeons have had actual clinical experience of the disease. It usually occurs in kittens and young adults, although at no age is the cat immune and as yet no effective vaccine has been produced.

The first signs are that the cat is lethargic and not very interested in its food. The coat may look 'open'. The rectal temperature varies from 102° to 107° F. and may swing in dramatic curves from day to day. As the disease progresses the cat obviously begins to lose weight (most noticeably along the spine) but the abdomen begins to swell, due to the secretion of fluid. Quite soon the cat has the appearance of a cat that is heavily in kitten. If the disease is untreated the terminal symptoms will begin to show. These are dehydration, diarrhoea (although the cat is usually constipated in the early stages) and finally difficulty in respiration and jaundice due to the break-down of the liver function.

Since the disease is caused by a virus, there is no drug which can be said to 'cure' it. However, recoveries have been known, due to veterinary skill and devoted nursing. The Animal Health Trust reports that a frequent paracentesis (withdrawal of the peritoneal fluid through the peritoneal wall) is necessary. After this has been done the abdominal cavity is irrigated with a penicillin solution. The fluid that is withdrawn is typical of the disease and is a useful guide to diagnosis, as it is viscous and often contains small particles of fibrin. 115

The drug Tylosin has been found to have been helpful in those cases that have recovered, and the cortico-steroid drugs are also useful as a supportive therapy.

The cat will have to be kept in a warm atmosphere of about 70° F. and if necessary it will have to be force-fed three-hourly with a high-protein liquid food.

Since it is suspected that feline infectious peritonitis is spread by insects that bite the owner is advised to take particular care to make sure that all the cats are free of both fleas and flea-eggs.

Worms. I have dealt in an earlier chapter with the problem of round-worms. However, many cats (though few kittens) may pick up tape-worms through an intermediate host, such as a dead mouse or bird, or fleas, or even garden-slugs. These hosts carry the intermediate stages of the tapeworm. Tapeworms are long, flat and segmented, and their heads are buried in the walls of the intestines. They can cause severe debility and loss of weight.

The first signs of a tapeworm are an open 'staring' coat, bad breath and a ravenous appetite. If the rear end of the cat is examined there will probably be something that looks like a grain of rice sticking to the hair of the anus. This is, in fact, the dried segment of a worm. Until a short time ago de-worming for tapeworm was an unpleasant process, as the only drugs which could kill the head of the worm caused severe sickness. However, there are now new drugs available (which can be given without any fasting) which destroy the head of the tapeworm, and the rest of the worm is dissolved or passed out in the faeces. With these drugs there is no purging or vomiting. It is very important that all contents of the sanitary tray should be burnt to prevent possible re-infection. The dose of vermifuge should be repeated in a fortnight's time.

After worming the cat should be given a tonic, such as 'Vitavel' to build up the general health and vitamin deficiency.

Feline Influenza. This disease, which affects the upper respiratory tract, is very prevalent amongst cats of all ages. It is not, as a rule, a fatal illness, but it can be very difficult to cure, and if very young kittens are affected pneumonia may often set in, resulting in death.

Symptoms: Often a cat or kitten may not even lose its appetite, but it will develop 'sniffles' and sometimes watering eyes. These 'sniffles' may become a mucous nasal discharge and the watering eyes may become pus-filled. There may be frequent sneezing, often accompanied by a cough. The temperature may be raised to 104° F., but it may remain near normal.

A really severe case of flu may result in a persistent dribble of saliva from the mouth and the eyes may develop conjunctivitis, when the conjunctivae become red and swollen. The disease is extremely infectious and one sneeze can cause an outbreak throughout a cattery.

Unfortunately, since research has shown that about 60 different types of virus cause influenzal symptoms, it has not been possible to produce a vaccine against this illness. A veterinary surgeon should be consulted at once, as he will be able to give drugs to counteract any secondary conditions such as pneumonia. It has even been found that the flu virus can travel to the reproductive system and be the cause of infertility, so it is especially necessary to give all possible treatment.

The sick cat should be isolated from all others and should remain in isolation for three weeks after recovery, as the virus has been known to remain active for three weeks. All swabs from infected nostrils and eyes should be carefully burnt, as the infection is also carried by these discharges.

As in all illnesses, the cat's nutrition should be kept at as high a level as possible, and it should be force-fed with liquids if it cannot take them voluntarily. The cat will be very distressed, as it will hate to feel messy, and it will need all the love and reassurance that its owner can give.

Ulcerative Glossitis is a condition where the cat's tongue is covered with small painful ulcers. It may be allied to influenza or may appear without any other cause, due to a virus infection. Often it is noticed after the cat has been to a show. The cat appears to be in some pain and is of course unwilling to eat or drink. The veterinary surgeon will give treatment by drugs and the cat's diet must be liquid until the condition has cleared.

Stomatitis is the medical term for ulcers affecting both tongue and all mucous membranes of the cat's mouth. It is very similar to glossitis and should be treated in the same way. Both these illnesses are infectious and the cat should be isolated and nursed with great care to avoid the spread of infection to other animals.

Skin Diseases. Fortunately, these cats are not prone to skin diseases, though there is one common condition in Rex cats which is not a disease, but is very disfiguring. This is loss of hair in patches over the body, giving the cat a very peculiar look and causing people to say 'The poor thing has mange.' One of my studs was affected like this and I was at a loss to know what to do, as tonics seemed of no use. Then my veterinary surgeon produced the theory that Rex cats, because they lose body-heat more quickly than normal cats, 117 need added fat to keep a good coat. I started giving a dessertspoon of shredded suet daily and after a month the cat's coat improved tremendously. Since this time all my Rex cats are automatically given extra fat, and they are all well-covered. The Colour-point-Rex-Coated and A.O.V. Club now issues this advice to all Rex breeders.

Ringworm. If a cat comes into contact with the ringworm fungus, it will be almost certain to contract the infection, and the tell-tale round bare patches of skin will appear. The patches are usually covered with dry skin, giving the appearance of cigarette ash. Not so long ago a cattery that had an outbreak of ringworm would have had the sufferers put to sleep, because it was almost impossible to cure. Now an antibiotic called 'Griseofulvin' is given by mouth and is a sure cure. However, all cats must be treated and all loose hairs carefully burnt as well as the cat's bedding, and the room carefully scrubbed out. The fungus has been known to live on a single hair for several years. Before a cat can be certified as being clear of infection, it will probably be put under a Wood's Lamp. This lamp is a form of ultra-violet light and any infected hair will glow with an almost unearthly brilliance beneath the light.

Parasites

Fleas and Lice: In spite of every care cats can easily pick up fleas or lice (these are tiny, grey-coloured tick-like creatures) and they can cause much irritation. They are also the intermediate hosts of the tapeworm and as such are a danger to health. The cat's coat should be regularly checked with a flea-comb for any insect and should be dusted with a good make of insect powder. It is important to make sure that the insect powder is made especially for cats, as any powder containing D.D.T. is extremely poisonous to cats.

Ear Mite: This is much more common than is generally supposed. It is a small mite that is almost impossible to see with the naked eye. It buries itself deep in the folds of the ear where it quickly multiplies. The cat's ears should be cleaned weekly with a cleaning agent supplied by the veterinary surgeon and applied on a Johnson's cotton-bud. If instead of a honey-coloured wax (which is normal) a dark wax shows on the swab it is an indication that the cat has ear-mite. This can be cleared fairly easily with a special liquid obtained from the veterinarian, but the ear must be treated regularly. Many people say 'my cat cannot have canker' (the common name for mite infection) 'as it doesn't scratch or shake its head.' But a cat will scratch only if the mite is already present in very large numbers. It is best to deal

118

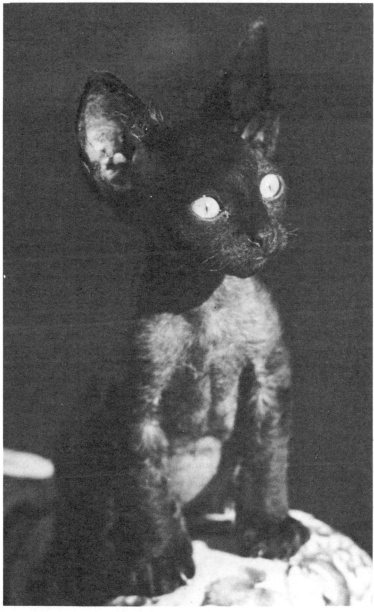

Ch. Hussan Truffles as a kitten (Devon). Owned and bred by Mrs. M.
Shrouder   *Photographer Arthur Shrouder*

with it in the early stage, before the cat has had a chance to suffer.

Mange: There are three types of mange, Sarcoptic, Notoedric and Follicular. All are caused by a mite which burrows into the skin. The cat suffers great irritation, scratching itself until the area becomes raw. The hair falls out and scaly scabs form. The cat is a sorry sight at this stage.

No type of mange is common, but notoedric and sarcoptic mange are slightly more common, though they are more easy to cure. Mange is very contagious and should betreated at the first sign by a veterinary surgeon. The cat must be isolated and the 'nurse' must be very careful to scrub well after treating the cat, as it is a disease which can be spread to humans. As with ringworm, all bedding must be burnt and the room disinfected.

A chapter on feline ailments would not be complete without mention of the Feline Advisory Bureau. This is a non-profit making organisation formed in 1958 by Mrs. Joan Judd. For an annual subscription of £1.50 anyone interested in cat welfare is entitled to free veterinary advice from an advisory panel of Britain's most eminent veterinary surgeons and geneticists. Leaflets on every aspect of cat-care are available for a nominal price and members also have access to a wide variety of books on scientific and genetic matters. The Bureau issues a quarterly magazine, which contains up-to-date news of feline ailments and their treatment. Allied to the Feline Advisory Bureau is the Central Fund for Feline Research, a registered charity which urgently needs funds. To date it has sponsored the work of research on Feline Respiratory Viruses by Dr. Johnson Ph.D., M.R.C.V.S., and Dr. C. Povey, Ph.D., M.R.C.V.S., and research on Feline Viral Peritonitis by G. Wilkinson, M.V.Sc., M.R.C.V.S. Further details can be obtained from Mrs. Joan Judd, The Barn Cottage, Tytherington, Wolton-under-Edge, Gloucestershire. GL12 8UG.

Ideal type Cornish Rex Head

Ideal type Devon Rex Head

Line drawings by Malcolm Lauder, M.R.C.

The first Siamese Pointed Devon Rex Kittens. Bred by Mrs. Lidyard

Photographer Derek Davis

Alison Ashford with Britain's first White Cornish Rex

Photographer Sloman & Pettitt

Index

Index